Big Steps, Long Strides

Andy, you're going to have this experience. I have every faith you will bring that medal home! Your time is Now!

Nisha

Big Steps, Long Strides

A Complete Guide to Running the Marathon des Sables

Nisha Harish

Foreword by Sir Ranulph Fiennes

Copyright © 2016 Nisha Harish
All rights reserved. No part of this publication may be reproduced, distributed or transmitted in any form or by any means, including photocopying, recording, or other electronic or mechanical methods, without the prior written permission of the author.
ISBN: 1519629974
ISBN 13: 9781519629975

"Whatever you can do, or dream you can do, begin it. Boldness has genius, power, and magic in it. Begin it now."
Johann Wolfgang von Goethe (1749–1832)

DEDICATION

The Finnish word "*Sisu*", (pronounced *See-Suu*), best encapsulates what it takes to run the Marathon des Sables.

Sisu is said to define the very essence of Finnish culture, yet its meaning is such that it cannot be embodied by any one word when translated into English. More than just "having guts" and distinct from persistence or drive, *Sisu* is something we all possess and is found at the end of our comfort zone, after we have exhausted grit and determination.

Sisu is special because it enables extraordinary, almost superhuman achievement, thereby contributing to what is often referred to as the action mind-set - or in other words, a consistent, courageous approach towards that challenge, which at first seems to exceed our abilities.

This book is dedicated to those who want to awaken their own *Sisu*. If you are to run the Marathon des Sables, you will need it.

CONTENTS

	Foreword	xi
	Acknowledgements	xiii
1	My Journey to the Sahara	1
2	About this Book	15
3	The Marathon des Sables	17
4	Training Strategy	23
5	What To Carry	39
6	What to Wear	55
7	Food & Hydration	59
8	Injury Prevention & Management	69
9	Pre-Race Preparation	75
10	Race Countdown & Completion	81
	Epilogue	91
	Resources	95
	Appendix A: Example Training Plan	101
	Appendix B: Example Key Milestone Plan	105
	Appendix C: Example Kit List	109
	Appendix D: Example Menu Breakdown	111
	Appendix E: Photographs	113
	Table of Figures	119
	Index	121

FOREWORD

For over 40 years, I have undertaken expeditions through a number of extreme environments. I am certain that the Sahara Desert is the harshest of them all.

Imagine running on a treadmill in the heat. Now imagine that there is no option to stop. The sun is making your head pound; your eyes are caked in tears mixed with sand, while the weight of your rucksack is dragging you down. One step forward means four steps back. All you can see for miles around you is sand dune after sand dune.

The blistering heat has resulted in dry, cracked lips and you have a pounding headache and a strange disorientation that simply cannot be fixed by the tepid water you are carrying. The wind is blowing but it somehow makes things worse, engulfing you in a wave of crushing heat.

Your blood pressure is rising from the heat, leaving you at risk of dizziness and fainting while your heart attempts to maintain adequate circulation. This can lead to confused, hostile or seemingly intoxicated behaviour, and the worst case scenarios include unconsciousness, multiple organ failure and in some cases, even death.

In this inhospitable environment, great friendships are forged. You need all the support you can get. Your survival depends on your own quick thinking: are you becoming dehydrated? Do you feel a drop in blood sugar levels? Do you need to eat something? Can you feel the loosening of another toenail? There is no room for squeamishness as you are left to lance your own blisters and tend to your own needs. Yet, somewhere in the depths of the Sahara, your true character emerges. It has to, because there is no place to hide. It's you against the environment- or rather, your ability to work *with* the environment. You must prepare well.

This guide will be an invaluable resource for you during your race preparation. In fact, you have a competitive advantage which you may not recognise until after successfully completing the race. The material contained within these pages is not only the capture of information, but represents invaluable knowledge that can only arise from lessons that have been hard-earned.

My lasting memory of the Marathon des Sables is one of intense hardship, but in the words of Winston Churchill, *"If you're going through hell, keep going."*

If you're lucky, you may even be kissed by a small Indo-Welsh woman along the way.

Sir Ranulph Fiennes

ACKNOWLEDGEMENTS

There are many people who have helped me on my journey to completing the Marathon des Sables. I would like to express my love and gratitude to my parents, who despite not understanding my desire for extreme and sometimes eccentric challenges, have never attempted to dissuade me, but instead have actively supported me in too many ways to mention. I do not take for granted that you are and always will be my biggest support system.

Thanks to my friend Simon Stead, with whom I have run many races and who ran the Marathon des Sables with me for the first time in 2014. Simon was too severely injured to return for a second attempt of the race in 2015, but despite this, he still came to Morocco to support me; a gesture I will always appreciate. Simon, you are probably the most optimistic person I know, with a remarkable ability to frame the most unfortunate of events in a positive light. I am grateful that this trait has rubbed off on me. I am grateful for you.

I have many friends who supported me in raising money for charity and who wrote to me while I suffered the trauma of the Sahara Desert - not once, but twice!

Thanks to my friend Paul Beagley ("Beagles"), who acted as a confidante during my training and later replayed how surreal it felt to receive an SOS text message from me, via the Sahara, on a rainy afternoon in the UK, when Simon and I got lost and then separated. Paul, you were my rock when I really needed you. Thank you.

I would also like to thank my former colleague and friend, Jackie Westbury, who was audacious in helping to raise as much money as possible for Macmillan Cancer Support. I love that "audacity" is a quality we share!

Thank you to my friends Helen Smith and Sarah ("Wild Thang") Wilding, who supported Simon and I through those long, arduous, 50-mile hikes. Thank you also to Alexander Bottom ("Botty") for your humour, which always makes me smile.

Thank you to my friend Hannah Paine, who blew me away by baking me a very special Marathon des Sables cake, the memory of which still makes me feel loved and supported all over again. Hannah, it goes without saying that without your help in editing, proofing and publishing this book, my lessons learned may never have been shared. If I were a man, I would actively pursue you and make you mine, because you are *just* perfect!

Thanks to Rodney Cullen, who's parting words, "*To even get to the start line is achievement alone,*" helped me to later reframe my initial failed attempt at the race.

Sid "*Running is Magic*" Wills, thank you for starting me on my running journey. I am one of many whom you continue to inspire. Thanks to my friend Paul Worsfold, a sports masseur whose healing hands helped me manage my injuries not once, but twice.

Thank you to my friends Nathan Whittaker and Brie Emmerson. Nathan helped me through the training required for my second attempt at the Marathon des Sables, by arranging plenty of varied, strenuous and beautifully scenic hikes through different parts of the UK. At times when I was demotivated and needed someone to tell me to go out for yet another training run, Nathan would text me, *"Go on, Nish! You can do it!"* It was just the support I needed.

My lovely friend Brie helped me in so many ways. On one occasion, Brie massaged my feet without my even asking, after a particularly hard run. Brie also joined me in the last ten miles of a 50-mile run and even created bespoke breakfast "Brie bars" for the duration of the race. Thank you for your love and for introducing me to the Finnish *Sisu*. I'm so grateful to have you in my life and close to my heart.

Thank you to my friends Jeff Hughes, Bert Lathrop, Michael ("Mikey") Kinghan, Sue Josephs, Liz Middlebrook, and Ray MacSweeney, who have always supported me with the right words of encouragement, irrespective of the nature of the challenge.

I would like to thank the Marathon des Sables organisation - specifically, my knight in shining Land Rover, Steve Dietrich, who found Simon alive and well during my first attempt at the race and who supported me through every check point of my second attempt with plenty of hugs and kisses. Thank you also to Sarah Chard, who recognised my "unfinished business" and supported my decision to attempt the race again.

The creation of this book has truly been a group effort, with so many friends, colleagues and acquaintances helping me in a variety of ways, from as far afield as the USA, Australia and Switzerland. Had it not been for Leigh Michelmore, a fellow runner from South Africa, who caught me as I was throwing up whilst hanging precariously over the side of a jebel, I may not have made it back!

Genis Pieterse, if you are reading this, please know that your studies have been invaluable in helping me develop some of my own thinking. Thank you for being so generous with your research and experience.

I would like to extend my heartfelt thanks to Kevin Houghton, Palma ("Ma") Giordano, Matthias Röser, Cheryl Richards, Alistair Fletcher, Nicky Matcham, Neil Hanham, Sarah Boucher and Norbert Van Der Neut, who acted as reviewers for specific aspects of this book, and Justine Talbot, who completed the final review. I would also like to thank my friends Mark Burnett and S-J Williams for their ongoing support – sometimes, just listening is enough!

Finally, to my best friend Sumeet Kapoor; thank you for being my sounding board in so many areas of life and for making me a better, more rounded person.

I sincerely hope that you, dear reader, receive all the support you need to help you through the gruelling training demands of the Marathon des Sables. You will find that you inadvertently inspire so many people who will want to be part of your journey by helping you in every way possible. There are times when you will doubt your own mental and physical abilities. It is at these times that you will need to put your faith in the hands of your loved ones because they will believe in you, even when you are losing faith in yourself. Enjoy the whole experience, for our willingness to believe in others surely represents one of the best qualities of the human spirit.

CHAPTER 1

MY JOURNEY TO THE SAHARA

How I Became a Runner

As a teenager growing up in South Wales, fitness did not feature in my life at all. I am British of Indian descent, so culturally there was less focus on anything extra-curricular and a greater focus on studying to get an education that would lead to a professional career. I was an inactive, chubby teenager and disliked anything remotely sport-related. In fact, my friend Clare and I would skip Physical Education classes at school and instead spend time talking about our growing crush on our English teacher, Mr. Kearns.

In my twenties, I was an average gym-goer. I would attend various classes such as body pump, circuits and aerobics. I maintained a regular weight training regime, having gleaned tips and advice from friends and perhaps obscurely, from *Men's Health* magazine. In the three years that I had been going to the gym, I had lost almost three stones in weight, so like many people, my primary motivation for exercising was to maintain a constant weight. Overall, my attitude towards exercising was that it was something I *should* do because it was good for me, rather than something I found especially enjoyable.

In terms of my running experience, at the very most, I would run for 20 minutes and that too, on a treadmill in walk-run intervals. Nevertheless, I considered myself to be reasonably fit and was proud that I had some degree of discipline - or to be precise, more discipline than most of the people in my social circle at the time.

During my late twenties, I lived in East London and worked in Central London as a Management Consultant. My life was busy and as my career progressed, it became increasingly stressful.

Having obtained the obligatory university education, a high-flying career and a foot on the elusive London property ladder, the only thing left on my "life list" was to marry and start a family. However, the end of a relationship, followed by the sudden and shocking deaths of six friends within a few months of each other, forced me to fundamentally re-evaluate my life. I found that despite having done all the "right" things, in the "right" order, the nagging question in my mind was, *"Is this it?"*

I felt that my life was like a never-ending conveyor belt. Although I had met one major milestone after another, such as acquiring an education, joining a profession and owning a property, I was unfulfilled. I wanted to travel and more than anything, I wanted to achieve extraordinary things. However, my recent experiences of death, along with my constant self-questioning and self-doubt led to low-level anxiety. I found that although exercise helped me to manage my weight, it wasn't really helping me to manage increasing stress levels.

I became increasingly conscious about time passing and had a persistent feeling that I was failing to reach my true potential. My mind was constantly in overdrive - so much so that I became an insomniac. I experienced knots in my stomach so frequently that I thought it was normal to feel that way. I would suffer panic attacks from being around large groups of people, including work colleagues and friends.

I remember on one occasion at work, as I stood in the doorway of the meeting room and surveyed the people in the room, I started to shake. My throat was dry and I could literally feel it constricting. I tried to calm my mind, but its internal chatter was telling me, *"They won't be interested in what you have to say. You're inexperienced. What do you know?"* I looked for an empty seat and sat down. I just wanted to be invisible and blend into the furniture. Even when I finally found the courage to speak, my voice was embarrassingly shaky and barely audible. I now know that I desperately lacked self-esteem.

Something had to be done, because collectively, these experiences began to affect my entire quality of life. My general feelings of inadequacy and underachievement, along with the feeling of time passing by were troubling me the most.

I needed to calm my mind and gain some control over my thoughts. I reasoned that if I could control my thoughts, I would be able to manage my emotions and thereby change the results in specific areas of my life. This in turn would reduce my anxiety. I guess this explains why I thought about exploring meditation. Since I didn't know *how* to meditate, I joined a group for those who were new to meditation, but I quickly realised that the spiritual angle that many of these groups promoted was not what I was looking for.

As I explored ways of managing anxiety and stress, I came across a magazine article which suggested that certain types of exercise, such as running, cycling and weight training, were sometimes regarded as physical forms of meditation because they induce a sense of "flow". Defined by the Mihaly Csikszentmihalyi, (Me-Hi-Eee Chick-Sent-Me-Hi-Eee), a professor of positive psychology, "flow", also known as "the zone", is the mental state of peak performance, where a person carrying out an activity is fully immersed in a feeling of energised focus, full involvement and enjoyment in the process of the activity. I think of this mental state as our "sweet spot", where we have both great strength and great ease; it is the mental state where our best work emerges without strain or anxiety. The ancient Chinese philosopher Lao Tzu called it "doing without doing" or "trying without trying".

You may have experienced it while driving or during any other routine activity that requires your full attention in such a way that you no longer experience the passing of time. Your mind and body are so calm that you begin to relax into a perfect state of harmony and synchronisation.

My Running History

It was against this backdrop that I developed a strong desire to explore a way of calming my mind. One day, a friend suggested that we should go for a short, four-mile run. This was my first experience of running outdoors - and one I will never forget.

I could barely even manage to run for 10 minutes. From the moment I started to run, my breathing and internal dialogue became chaotic. If you are new to running, or indeed even if you are an accomplished runner, you will recognise that your internal monologue can start to go crazy. For me, it went something like this: *"This is painful. I can't breathe. I should have worn another layer. Ah, cute dog. I wonder what I'll have for dinner. It's so cold. I think I'll have pasta. I think I'm slowly dying."*

Buddhists call this mental ping-pong game "monkey mind", referring to the random musings that bounce around your head. Although my friend kept talking to me to distract me from the discomfort, I just could not focus. It was as though my body and mind were completely disjointed and at odds with one another. I gave up and walked home, defeated, while my friend continued his run without me. I felt ashamed, a feeling that was exacerbated by my already unhappy state of mind.

I was tired of feeling so low, so I guess you could say that this was my tipping point. The desire to manage my thoughts, through the exploration of running as a physical form of meditation, was what spurred me on. I resolved to use running as a way of synchronising my body and mind so that they were in harmony.

Initially, I focused on making the act of going for a run a regular part of my weekly routine. I ignored concerns about time or distance. I ran from my front door to the first lamp post on my street. I then built this up to the second lamp post, then the third and so on until eventually, I was comfortably running three miles. These early runs and indeed many more subsequent runs, were characterised by a mixed walk-run strategy. I experienced good days of happy runs and bad days of not-so-happy runs. I wanted to learn how to get into a "flow" state, so I focused on relaxing my muscles, regulating my breathing and acknowledging my feelings. As I began to notice the wind in my hair and the sun on my face, my mind began to calm.

I found the first 30 minutes of a run to be the most difficult, after which the initial discomfort would slowly subside. As my mileage increased, albeit incrementally at first, so did my self-esteem. The very act of being in motion was helping me to manage my emotions.

The runner and journalist, Kristin Armstrong, once said that, *"There is something magical about running; after a certain distance, it transcends the body. Then a bit further, it transcends the mind. A bit further yet, and what you have before you, laid bare, is the soul."* This was exactly the effect that running was having on me. It was imperceptible at first, but over time, I began to feel mentally and physically stronger.

I suppose the increased confidence is what gave me the impetus to join some colleagues for a weekly lunchtime run. However, I quickly learned that I preferred to run alone - partly because this promoted my desire to calm my mind, but mostly because I felt that trying to maintain a conversation while exerting myself was just too difficult for me.

Nevertheless, one of these colleagues suggested that I needed a goal and encouraged me to register for a 5km race. If you live in the UK, you may know that there are a number of races, known as "Race for Life", that are organised by the charity, Cancer Research. I registered for my first race and found that I loved the feeling of being a part of that experience.

Many people were running in memory of a loved one and had written signs on the back of their t-shirts, explaining who they were running for and why. I remembered the friends I had lost and often became quite emotional. We were all in the same boat and running with these people made me feel that I was part of something positive and bigger than just myself.

I ran more and more, registering for one race after another. As my anxieties became better managed, I felt compelled to keep exploring my boundaries. I developed distinct preferences, such as running in the morning before work, listening to specific types of music for particular types of runs and perhaps most bizarrely, running around the periphery of the royal parks of London on the concrete pavement, rather than taking a more scenic route inside the parks.

As my routine became more established, my friends, family and colleagues began identifying me as a runner and my courage grew. I was no longer interested in the gym because that was not where I felt most challenged. Instead, I looked for goals, which in hindsight helped to reinforce my new-found positive self-image. I joined the London-based Serpentine Running Club and enrolled in a running course for beginners, which taught running technique.

The course was led by Sid Wills, a tall, slim 68-year old man. Originally from Newcastle, with a Geordie accent and a warm, affable style, Sid's dedication to running and coaching new runners moved me. I reasoned that if Sid could run half marathons, why couldn't I? I was inspired. My next goal was to run a half-marathon.

All of these elements represent my early running journey, but none quite explain how or why I decided to enter the Marathon des Sables.

One Sunday afternoon, during lunch with my friend Steve - a year or so before I had plucked up the courage to run my first marathon, the conversation turned to goals and aspirations. Steve described what is known as the toughest footrace on earth: the Marathon des Sables. He went on to explain the details of the 156-mile ultra-marathon and described it as the 'ultimate test of self-sufficiency'. The race captured my imagination like nothing before. I was enthralled.

At that point, it didn't occur to me that the Marathon des Sables could be something that I could do. It just seemed too distant in terms of where I was in my running experience and although my confidence was improving, I didn't have enough courage.

I went on to run several half marathons and as I did so, the idea of running the 26.2 miles required for a marathon seemed less elusive. Other runners began to tell me that if I could run a half marathon, a marathon was eminently achievable. I began to dream. If I had the opportunity to run a marathon - *any* marathon, which would I run?

My First Marathon

Since I lived in London, all of my marathon training would be London-based, but I wanted to run my first marathon in another great city. I wanted to create a memorable experience that would stay with me for the rest of my life. After all, I was only intending to run one marathon. I decided to run the New York Marathon because I thought the crowd support and the city landscape would make this race a unique and memorable experience for me.

In hindsight, I suppose that it was already a bold step to run my first marathon alone, in a city that was completely unknown to me. However, by this point, I had become so used to running by myself that the prospect of being lonely during a marathon didn't even occur to me and I received so much invaluable support once I announced my entry to friends, family and colleagues.

I began to build up my mileage very slowly; running through cold, bitter conditions and through pitch-black darkness and rain. During those long runs, I'd sometimes feel defeated. Recognising that the run was not working as planned - perhaps due to a blister or unfamiliar and worrying pain, I would abort the run, but I would always try again. I did not want to be the kind of person who would give up. That mind-set has become part of the make-up of my personality today. It would fuel me to run 10 miles or more, sometimes before work. In fact, at the peak of my marathon training, I once even ran 20 miles before work and for the first time in my life, I felt invincible.

For me, running a marathon was a profound experience. It's quite strange to be running in one direction with 47,000 people from different countries and backgrounds, with the single aim of crossing the finish line.

I remember one particular point in the race, when I was almost doubled over in pain; my knees were very sore and I could see that they were gradually swelling up. I slowly stood up straight and saw to my right, just over the barrier, an overweight man, dressed in a cop's uniform, clutching a doughnut in one hand and pushing his way to the front of the crowd. He started angrily punching the air with his right hand and in a distinctive Brooklyn accent, screamed, *"Lady, don't you stop! You CAN do this!! You OWN this* road!!!" I felt overwhelmed that this man, a complete stranger who didn't even know me, believed that I could finish the race. Moments such as this were so emotional that even now, years afterwards, they still bring a lump to my throat and tears to my eyes. In the face of such encouragement, how could I not pick myself up and carry on?

As I ran through the boroughs of the city, with the encouragement of thousands of people watching, clapping and screaming my name to keep going, I felt lifted. The New York marathon was an outstanding experience and even today it remains my favourite race. I had also raised almost £3,000 for charity by running just this one race.

As I crossed the finish line, I felt an enormous sense of loss and almost despair. It was all over. I had learned so much and evolved so much. What would I do now?

Several days after completing my first marathon, some friends asked me how I felt about having completed my first marathon. I replied that in spite of feeling a sense of achievement, I also felt that I had lost my sense of purpose. My friends were supportive, but a day or so later I received an email from my friend Kevin, which left a lasting impression for several years afterwards. This is what he wrote:

"So, are you recovered now? And what's this about post-marathon blues? You have a lot to learn. This could be just the beginning. I can't tell you what goal to pick. The choice is yours. And what a choice! A marathon, a half, a 10 miler, a 10k...a 4-minute mile????? Errr...ok let's make that a 6-minute mile. Now pause and remember what you have done. Something I can only wish for. You've run the New York marathon. You are a marathon runner now. Welcome to the club; a club you will always be a member of."

It was then that I realised that I didn't need to stop. The New York marathon really could be the beginning of my journey, rather than the culmination of many months of training to get to an end-point. I don't think Kevin ever imagined the profound impact his words would have on me.

After My First Marathon

The connectedness of thousands of people and being part of that amazing energy is the closest to a spiritual experience that I have ever had. In fact, in almost every race I have ever run, I have felt sudden tearfulness almost as an impromptu reaction from the enormity of the experience. This goes some way toward explaining why I went on to run so many more marathons.

I wanted to run memorable races and create unique experiences. I ran marathons in Berlin, Paris and Amsterdam, to name a few. In fact, before I knew it, I had registered for 10 marathons in 10 months. There was no doubt that I was addicted to the endorphins, however, running made me feel good for so many more reasons.

Gradually, I became aware that although running had improved my self-esteem, I was still lacking in confidence. This would manifest itself particularly at work, when I had to lead a meeting or give a presentation. I didn't have a problem delivering the content I was intending to talk about, but I was fearful of speaking up. I imagined that my audience was judging me as being incapable.

I didn't want to be scared anymore; my fear was emotionally exhausting. I started to think creatively about how I might resolve this issue. I reasoned that if I didn't resolve it, this issue would become progressively worse and over time, would adversely impact my overall quality of life. I came to the conclusion that

I needed to do something so scary that any other challenge by comparison would pale into insignificance; I needed to take extreme measures.

Personally, I can think of few things scarier than performing as a stand-up comic. I decided that that was what I would do - I would train to become a comic and then use my stand-up comedy skills not only to build confidence in the work place, but also to support my fundraising efforts. Since I had now run many sponsored races, my friends, family and colleagues were reaching charity fatigue. I acknowledged that it was unreasonable for me to keep asking for sponsorship for something that I could now do with relative ease, without offering something in return.

I remember going into work and telling my friend Malcolm about my audacious plan. He looked at me as though I had gone crazy. It *was* a crazy idea, but by this point, instead of thinking that I could not do something, I began to question *why* I couldn't. I had also reached a point where I felt that I had nothing to lose. I was desperate to change.

I trained with a comedy club based in Camden every Saturday for three months along with Willie, a police officer and former client who had become a friend.

I decided to perform stand-up comedy gigs for my work colleagues and corporate clients. I decided on corporate clients specifically, because this would address my fear of speaking in a corporate environment, but also, since I worked for EY, they would match any money that I raised for various charitable causes. Performing in front of audiences over and over again meant that my confidence grew exponentially. Even when I once "died" on stage - forgetting my comedy material, I learned to pick myself up and carry on. Within six months, I had worked my way up to perform stand-up comedy to an audience of more than 250 people, many of whom were my colleagues and clients. This experience not only addressed my fear, but also helped me to raise huge amounts of money for charity, alongside the running.

Following my experiences of running the New York marathon and taking in the amazing sites, I was inspired to run the Paris Marathon.

It was a beautiful marathon and a unique experience. I remember around two hours into the race, my internal dialogue began a cycle of negative questioning, asking, *"Why am I even here? When is this going to stop?"* Suddenly, I felt a tap on my right shoulder. As I turned, I saw that it was a man carrying a horn. I later learned that in most marathons, when there is a vulnerable person running, such as an elderly or blind person, they are usually flanked by more experienced runners who act as support. In this instance, the man was pushing what looked like a makeshift hospital bed. There were two men at the bottom of the bed, pulling it and one man on the right hand side of the bed, pushing it. On the bed itself, lay a young girl, probably around 10 or 12 years old. I slowed down. Looking at the bed and then at the man, I asked, *"Why are you pushing her?"* He explained that the girl was his sister and that she had terminal cancer. Before her death, she wanted to experience what it was like to be part of a marathon, so the man, his father and two brothers had all trained together to help the little girl reach the finish line. Re-telling this story brings me close to tears every time. I have so many stories like this that have continued to inspire me, even to this day.

Marathons gave me a sense of belonging and a connectedness to the positive aspects of the human spirit. I have so many wonderful, shared experiences with fellow runners from all over the world that make me proud to be part of the running sub-culture.

One of my favourite memories was when I ran the Marathon du Medoc in Bordeaux with my friend, Pete. This was a special running event, which seemed to actively encourage everything that is normally discouraged for runners. Held every September in France's Médoc region, it is possibly the most ridiculous marathon known to man. The course is 26.2 miles through scenic vineyards and the runners - in compulsory fancy dress, are expected to indulge in 23 glasses of the famed vintages en route, while also stuffing themselves with local specialities such as oysters, foie gras, cheese, steak and ice-cream. It sounded so absurd that I definitely wanted to be part of it.

My next marathon was across the Great Wall of China. It was at London's Gatwick Airport, and it was as I stood in line for check-in that a lean, bald man in his mid-forties smiled at me. Recognising our matching luggage tags, we realised that we were part of the same tour group, and began talking. He told me that his name was Simon and that he was travelling with his friend, Danny. I didn't really feel like talking, especially when he asked me, *"Are you doing the full marathon, then?"* In my typically defensive style, I responded with, *"Yeah. Why? Don't you think I can?"* As he hurriedly reassured me that his question was not intended to be a slight, I realised that I actually rather liked this mild man.

Days later, as I got to know him, I saw how soft and sensitive Simon was. When the group separated, he and Danny came to my room to say good-bye. As he handed me the gift of a Mars bar, his eyes were welling up with tears. He told me that he didn't expect us to ever meet again and that he knew he'd never take another trip like this one. This was categorically not true. Our friendship was established during that 12-day tour and we became good friends. In fact, Simon and I went on to run the Amsterdam and Barcelona marathons and even climbed to Mount Everest Base Camp together.

Although Simon was based in Manchester, we maintained our friendship through emails and phone calls. One of the particular quirks I like about Simon is that he always ends every phone call with, *"God bless."* How could I not remain friends with such a gentle man?

Perhaps my least favourite race was the Amsterdam marathon. Although the course is flat and popular among those looking to get a good marathon time, I found the organisation to be disappointing from the outset. Despite the bad start, one positive experience stands out. As I reached the 20-mile mark and started to feel generally sorry for myself, a man in a wheelchair slowed down to give me a bag of jelly babies. There's nothing quite like perspective, is there?

Throughout this time, I continued to perform stand-up comedy as a means of further fundraising. As the 10 marathons in 10 months challenge came to an end, I started to explore other challenges. I had developed an appetite for trying new things and didn't want to wait for "one day". I wanted to live with no regrets. To that end, I started to do all of the extra-curricular things I had wanted to do since childhood. I learned to play the saxophone, I tried snowboarding and fishing, I also climbed Mont Blanc, Kilimanjaro and did many, many other things. It was as Simon and I descended from Everest Base Camp that we started thinking about our next challenge. We wanted to run the toughest foot race on earth.

My First Experience of the Marathon des Sables

By the time Simon and I had decided to register for the Marathon des Sables, I had run numerous marathons and I recalled my introduction to the race through my conversation with my friend Steve several years earlier. I had reached a point where the dream of running across the Sahara was no longer out of my reach - at least not in my mind.

Simon and I registered for the race in 2014 and parted with significant sums of money for race entry, additional training races and kit for the actual race. For almost a whole year we hardly talked about anything else other than our much-anticipated challenge. We watched the British Olympic rower, James Cracknell's DVD, entitled *The Toughest Race on Earth* and would talk excitedly about what lay ahead.

When I shared my intentions with work colleagues, I received a tremendous amount of support. My former colleague and friend, Hannah Paine, even baked a cake that depicted the finish line at the Marathon des Sables. The cake was auctioned at work to raise money for Macmillan Cancer Support. Other colleagues sponsored me and offered a huge amount of encouragement. My friend and colleague, Paul Beagley, would leave a banana on my desk every Friday morning as reward for my long pre-work run. In total, we raised over £10,000 for Macmillan Cancer Support.

It's quite strange to try to explain the Marathon des Sables experience to someone who hasn't run it. It is more than just running. It also means a different way of life for a whole week. I was looking forward to life without email and social media, amongst other things. I was also curious to know how it would feel to be in the silence of the desert. I was, of course, fearful of the heat and I worried constantly about whether I had trained enough.

We set out to Morocco two days before the start of the race. Simon was planning to take a bus from Manchester directly to the airport, where I would meet him. As I arrived at Gatwick Airport, it was easy to spot the runners. Everyone carried their rucksacks, which contained their kit and food packs for seven days. Even more distinctive was the choice of footwear. Each runner wore their gaiters attached to their trainers, for fear of losing them in misplaced luggage.

Upon arrival in Morocco, we were greeted with several litres of water, a packed lunch and a six-hour bus trip to the camp. By the time we arrived at camp, it was almost 9pm and pitch-black. As the bus stopped, we were all advised to have our head torches in hand. Blinking nervously once the bus doors opened, we all descended and took a short walk into the strange semi-circle of black canvas tents, peppered with Berbers and camels.

Simon and I had made some friends at one of the stops en route to the camp. We had all agreed to share a tent, otherwise known as a bivouac (pronounced *Biv-Oo-Ac*). Although robust, these essentially consisted of a large sheet of black canvas nailed down into the ground and supported by wooden poles. I later learned that the Berbers would be taking these tents down and reassembling them at every stage.

Once we had established our preferred spot in our bivouac, all eight of us – seven men, five of whom were from the military, and myself – headed off to the main tent for dinner. Prior to the start of the race, runners were looked after in comparative luxury. It felt strange to be eating crusty bread, fresh yoghurt, spaghetti bolognaise with Parmesan cheese, creamy mushroom soup and even drinking red wine in the depths of the Sahara Desert. We had one more night like this until the official start of the race on Sunday. From that point onwards, we would be on our own and would have to be completely self-sufficient.

The next day, as we awoke groggy-eyed and took in the enormity of what lay before us, we were told the plan of events. We had to go through the logistics of medical sign-offs, kit check and our final bag pack. This day essentially involved all 1,300 or more nervous runners packing, unpacking and re-packing their kit into their rucksacks, ready for the start of the race.

The atmosphere was electric. If you have ever experienced running a marathon, imagine the excitement of standing at the start line and multiply it by a thousand.

There were a few speeches from Patrick Bauer, the race director, and plenty of live music. Once checks were complete and our kit was packed, Simon and I lay in our tent relaxing and watching the elite athletes talking easily with all other runners. It was hot, but not unbearably so, due to the gentle breeze. I enjoyed soaking up the atmosphere and felt immensely proud to have made it this far and to be with this group of people. I talked to absolutely everyone I could. After all, how many more opportunities would I have to meet people with such an alternative mind-set?

It felt as though we were at a festival rather than at the beginning of a terrifying race.

Each day started with a round-up of news from Patrick Bauer. The briefing included general information such as the race position achieved by the top elite athletes at each stage, the planned route details and the expected temperature for the day. Excitement was further increased with a daily rendition of ACDC's "*Highway to Hell*", played at the start line.

Lost in the Sahara

Our first day of the Marathon des Sables in 2014 was horrific. It was characterised by miles and miles of sand dunes higher than the eye could see. Simon and I couldn't keep up with the rest of the group due to the tremendous weight of our rucksacks and the difficulty of the terrain.

What made it much worse was that we couldn't see route markings once we entered the sand dunes. These factors contributed to us getting separated from the rest of the runners and it was then that we realised that neither Simon nor I knew how to use a compass. Instead, we agreed to follow two Japanese men just ahead of us, reasoning that Japanese tourists generally know what they're doing, so why wouldn't Japanese runners? One man was wearing a bright red afro-style wig, whilst the other thought it would be a wise decision to run across the Sahara in a woolly cow costume, despite the 56°C temperature.

Simon was faster than me and insisted on going further ahead to see the direction the other runners had taken. I was carrying around 15kg of dead weight on my back and felt completely and utterly overwhelmed. There was no way I could have run, even if I wanted to.

Realising that Simon was nowhere in sight, panic set in. I shouted his name, but I couldn't see him. I tried frantically to climb the sand dune above me. Up and up and up. But it was no good. The soft sand and the weight of my rucksack pulled me down. I pushed my way up and up and up and then screamed louder, "*Siiiiiiiiiiiiiiimonnn!!*". It was so strange to not hear an echo. I screamed again and for as long as I could. "Simoooooooooooooooooooooon!" My throat was parched. Ordinarily, I would have cursed him, but I was terrified. I knew he had less water than me. He could be lost. I tried to set off my distress flare, but it didn't work. In my panic I sent a text message to my friend Paul, back in the UK, "*Paul, emergency, need to pull out. Simon lost. Please text emergency whistle signal.*" For some unknown reason, I thought that Paul, a city professional might know the convention for sending an emergency whistle signal. Suddenly, my phone vibrated. It was Paul, "Serious???" Of course I was serious! I cursed Paul under my breath and put my phone away in frustration.

I needed more power in my legs. But the more I tried to push myself up the sand dunes, the harder it became. Focus. That's what I needed. "*Just focus, Nisha!!*" I told myself, "*You're becoming hysterical!*" How could an experienced marathoner become hysterical? What was going wrong? Too much heat and sun? Had I made a mistake somewhere? At that point, there simply wasn't enough time to think about what was going wrong. I remembered what I had learned about the concept of flow. I needed to relax.

"*Concentrate on your breath.*" That's what I would do. Concentrate. Then the seriousness of the situation hit me. The two Japanese men that I had been following had vanished. There was no one in sight. I was in the Sahara Desert, alone.

The sun, like a heat lamp, was burning the left side of my face and neck. The medium sized hat that I was wearing didn't fit me properly and kept blowing off. To top it all off, the neck curtain, which was supposed to protect the back of my neck from the sun didn't cover either sides of my face. I was slowly coming to the realisation that I had made some major errors in my kit selection.

All around me were sand dunes as high as my eyes could see. It was both picture-perfect and a living nightmare; sand dune after sand dune, perfect and untouched by footsteps. I couldn't see or hear anything. There was something wet trickling down my right leg. I wiped the back of my leg and looked at my hand, expecting to see blood, but no, it was sweat. I was sweating so profusely that I was shivering, yet at the same time, my head felt like it was being microwaved.

I lifted the waist belt of my rucksack to tried to re-distribute the weight higher on my hips, but it was no good. At 5"1, I was too small and the rucksack was too big and too heavy for my frame. It was day one of the race, which meant that I was carrying the maximum load of a whole seven days' worth of food.

I decided to listen to some music. As I put in my earphones, the music started. *"Copa…Copacabana, Music and passion were always in fashion At the Copa…Copacabana…"* To this day, I'm not sure what possessed me to think that listening to Barry Manilow in the Sahara Desert would be a good idea. I had planned a comprehensive music playlist, working on the premise that distraction would help me. I had everything from Barry White to gospel music, and even Hindu religious mantras.

"Move. Keep moving, Nisha," I thought to myself. But move to where? I carried on, slowly making my way up one sand dune only to realise that there were many, many more sand dunes ahead of me, irrespective of the direction I took.

Finally, in the distance, I could see that the sand dunes were coming to an end. I saw some distinctive black Berber bivouacs and some weird looking, malnourished camels with skinny, long legs that made them appear as though they were walking on stilts.

As I got closer, I started to see other runners.

I stopped and flagged them down. By this point I was almost hysterical *"Simon, have you seen Simon?"* I asked frantically, as though they must surely know who he was. I pleaded some more, becoming increasingly desperate, *"Please help me, I need to get to checkpoint one. Simon might be waiting for me. I've lost him."* They all shook their heads.

The terrain began to change. Instead of sand dunes, there was sporadic vegetation and gravel-like terrain. It was a weird experience. One minute I was in sand dunes, the next, it felt like I was in the Saharan equivalent of an empty backstreet car park. I saw more people making use of the flat terrain by walking or running as quickly as their legs would allow. I found that despite all I had learned about managing my mind and body through previous marathons, I was out of my depth. This was the first race that really challenged my body and my mind to the absolute limit.

"Checkpoint one? You've missed it. It was 5 miles that way", said one runner, pointing back the way I had just come. In utter desperation, I started the journey back towards checkpoint one. I was going in the opposite direction to the runners, but I had to go back because I simply didn't have enough water to carry me through the next 16km to check point two.

I got a mixture of reactions from the runners who saw me running towards them, in the opposite direction of every other runner. Some runners were very sorry and pitying, but one man even said what I'm sure many were thinking; *"How could you be so stupid?"*

How *could* I have been so stupid? I had wanted to do this race for 5 years. It had captured my imagination like nothing else I'd ever known or attempted. It sounds so irrational as I sit and write these words in a sanitary western environment without the effect of delirium, dehydration and 56°C heat, but I was terrified that Simon was lost and dying somewhere. As I walked 5 miles as fast as I could, back to check point one, I realised that Simon was not there. As I picked up my water rations, I ran to one of the race administrators.

"Madam, vous parlez anglais?" (*Madam, do you speak English?*)

"Oui, un peux, porquoi?" (*"Yes, a little, why?"*), she said, gently.

"Y at-il quelqu'un ici qui parle bien anglais?" (*"Is there someone who can speak English well?"*)

I was surprised at my own fluency, but embarrassed that I couldn't progress the conversation much further in French. Recognising my urgency, the lady called one of the doctors, "Mikael!! Viens ici!"

As Mikael began walking towards us I recognised him from Saturday. He was the doctor responsible for completing our kit checks and handing us mandatory equipment, such as salt tablets, that had been provided by the race administration.

Checking the records in his ring binder, he confirmed that he had no record of Simon. He then spoke to a colleague on a walkie-talkie and confirmed that Simon had not been identified at check point two, either. I didn't know what to do.

"You must start walking. You can still make it to the end of this stage, but you must hurry. Don't waste time. Go now!" Fear gripped me. I was terrified of not being able to find my way and getting lost again.

I picked up my walking poles and set off in the same direction I'd just come from. It was heart breaking because this time, as I walked to check point two, I saw no one. I was alone again.

It was at some point on the way to check point two that I met Steve Dietrich, who pulled up in a Land Rover. Steve was one of the race administrators; a lovely man with grey hair, an easy smile and kind, sparkly blue eyes. I explained that I had lost my friend and was worried about him. He said that he would search for Simon and told me to continue towards the camp.

As I resumed walking, my phone began to vibrate, I had received a text message from Paul, back in the UK! As I read it, I felt euphoric, *"Simon has time logged at checkpoint two but not checkpoint one so he might be on track. You keep going."*

I later learned that Paul had called Sarah, an MdS organiser who in turn, called Steve. Some time later, Steve pulled up alongside me as I was walking along the hot, dusty road and confirmed that Simon had reached checkpoint two. Fuelled by the news that my friend was alive and well, I continued marching. I was far, far behind the rest of the race at this point. It was almost 6pm and already getting dark. I had to pull out my head torch.

Hours later, Steve pulled up in his Land Rover again and said, *"Go quickly, Nisha. You're the last person to enter the sand dunes. Go quick!"*

It's a weird experience being in the Sahara and trying to climb sand dunes in pitch-black darkness. The race organisers had arranged green glow sticks to mark the route out of the sand dunes. These were helpful, but posed one major difficulty; I had no sense of distance and no idea where the glow sticks were sitting in relation to the sand dunes I was traversing. It would seem that the light was in front of me, but then I would be walking for what seemed like hours, before passing that light and seeing another.

Finally, I saw a huge green beam of light flooding the black, starlit sky, indicating the camp location. As I came closer to the finish line, I could just about make out Simon's shadowy silhouette. I don't think I've ever hugged anyone as hard as I hugged Simon that night.

Simon carried my rucksack and end-of-day water rations back to the tent and made sure that I had eaten sufficiently to recover from the trauma of the day. I checked my feet, carefully taking off my shoes and peeling off my socks. Surprisingly, at that point, I had only developed one blister.

Simon and I always remained together after this point. The variation of the terrain in the desert was surprising. In the Western world, when we think of the desert, we typically imagine lots of sand, yet what Simon and I experienced were lots of dried riverbeds, rocks, sand dunes, dunettes and village ruins.

On day two, we started to see the first casualties. One Japanese man was standing by a tree, apparently vomiting for the whole of Japan. Another guy sat convulsing along the valley bed. This routine was sadly pretty standard. In the blistering heat of the day, we would take a salt tablet and drink our water. And then drink a bit more just in case. And then eat, because we were paranoid at having had too much water and feared not having enough salt in our bodies. A couple of scorching hot valleys later, we began the last climb up a sandy ascent, followed by the first glimpse of camp, about 3km away.

The valley beds seemed to hold the heat of the day more so than the dunes and seemed like an alternative reality. I moved, but I didn't. I could see the trees in the distance, but they didn't come any closer.

I was very pleased to reach camp - this time with Simon, rather than alone. By now, the camp felt luxurious, as we were welcomed over the finish line with a hot cup of sweet Moroccan mint tea.

My nerves at the start line of day three were replaced by equal quantities of mild excitement and mild dread. Running the Marathon des Sables meant that all we could think about was the next checkpoint. My mind could not stray any further than the next checkpoint, because thinking too far ahead would induce fears that were utterly overwhelming.

I was growing increasingly worried about the effects of the heat, as one of our tent mates had unfortunately been pulled from the race. We found him on the evening of day two, grey with pulsing calf muscles. He was delirious. Seven intravenous drips later, he returned to our bivouac. He had tried to complete the early part of the day's race but was so dehydrated that he had needed another intravenous drip. It was game over for him.

On day three, as we left check point two, I remember asking Simon, *"How are you feeling, Si?" "Fine"*, he replied. We were both in good spirits. Physically, we agreed that we felt relatively good. I had developed seven or eight blisters and had noticed at least two toenails that were ready to fall off. We were still at the back of the race and as we approached the final checkpoint on day three, we saw a very serious looking Steve Dietrich, who told us with great sadness that we were to be pulled from the race, because we had no hope of reaching the finish line within the designated time limit.

We were devastated. It was not until we were actually taking part in the race that we realised that much of our hard work and preparation had been in vain. Although we trained often and hard, we did not prepare in the right way. In fact, our preparation in so many areas – foot care, nutrition, hydration, kit quantity, and kit choices – were absolutely ill informed and led to catastrophic results.

The problem was that, despite our collective experience of running more than 40 marathons, both Simon and I were overwhelmed by the amount of thinking and planning this race involved. Ultra-running; that is, any distance over the 26.2 miles required by a marathon, demands race strategy and training preparation that is distinct from marathon running. Similarly, multi-stage racing, which often involves running back-to-back marathons, requires a different strategy again. Simon and I had not taken these important distinctions into account when we devised our training approach for the Marathon des Sables.

This affected the way in which we went about our preparation, which had been haphazard, due to all of the unknown aspects of both the race and the environment.

Bill Gates once said that, *"Success is a lousy teacher. It seduces smart people into thinking they can't lose."* In my case, this was certainly true. Failing the Marathon des Sables at first attempt and then making the decision to go back and do it again was a real learning curve for me. Of course I had experienced failure before, but I had succeeded at so many outrageous challenges prior to the MdS that I was in shock. I actually couldn't believe it.

Having been pulled from the race, Simon and I were asked to wait in a bivouac at the checkpoint. As we entered the bivouac, we saw a much older South African woman and a Polish woman who had red eyes and a puffy face from crying so much. Almost as though he was reading my thoughts, Simon turned to me and said, *"We can't see this as failure, Nisha. This is feedback."* Simon's words stuck with me for months afterwards and encouraged me to reflect deeply on what had gone wrong and why.

We were driven back to the camp and shared our bad news with our tent mates. We were told that we would need to spend another night in the camp with the other runners. In the morning, we would be taken back to Ouarzazate. As Simon and I took the long journey to the hotel, I pulled out my phone and started to make a long list of all the things I would do differently if I were to run the race again. I didn't want to forget a single thing.

As runners arrived at the hotel following the race, I picked their brains for tips on strategy, training, kit, nutrition and hydration. I recorded every single technical aspect of my Marathon des Sables experience and subsequently tested out multiple ideas and theories relating to the race. I also recorded the things that I would definitely recommend other people *should* do. I went on to run the Marathon des Sables again and this time came back with the medal I knew I deserved, having fully tested the effectiveness of my revised preparation.

My desire to return to the Marathon des Sables was not due to fear of being perceived as a failure by other people, nor was it because I felt the need to prove myself to anyone other than myself. I suppose you could say that through my journey to completing the Marathon des Sables, I was actually building my character. My objective was to have one reference point in my life that proved to me beyond a shadow of doubt that I had the courage, drive and resilience to achieve something remarkable.

I hope that by sharing my journey, of how I went from being a non-runner to ultra-runner, you to see that anything is possible. I sincerely wish you all the luck in your preparation to run the Marathon des Sables. Actually, I take that back. Experience tells me that luck has nothing to do with it. Dig deep, find your own *Sisu*, and bring that medal home.

CHAPTER 2

ABOUT THIS BOOK

This book contains my lessons learned, having failed and then returned to complete the Marathon des Sables successfully. It is a technical guide that covers every aspect that you need to know about the race, irrespective of your experience as a runner.

Your experience currently may be limited to 5k, 10k or half marathon distances. Alternatively, you may be an experienced marathoner looking to make the jump to ultra-running. You may even be a well-established ultra-runner looking to run the MdS for the first time. Irrespective of your experience, this book presents a complete guide to running the Marathon des Sables.

It is my hope that the information contained here will save you from going through the training commitment, cost and trauma that I went through in 2014, only to return without a medal. If you train in the right way and do the correct preparation, you absolutely deserve a medal. This book aims to steer you in the right direction and I sincerely hope that it prevents you from making the same mistakes I made when I first ran the race.

What to Expect

This book is a guide for those people who have no experience of running the Marathon des Sables, or maybe even a marathon. It will be especially useful for you if you:

- have never run MdS before;
- are a first-time marathoner;
- have never run an ultra-marathon;
- have no experience of adventure racing;
- have little or no experience of multi-stage, multi-day racing;
- have no idea where to start in terms of training for an environment like the Sahara Desert;
- have no idea what kit to wear or what equipment to carry;
- are looking for guidance from someone with experience.

For most people, the commitment required to achieve a top 20 position is too substantial. To that end, this guide is aimed at those with more modest goals, which are more realistic given family, relationship, work and other commitments. This book will be particularly useful to you if you want to simply complete the race.

Disclaimer

This book has been written with the assumption that you have little or no experience of running a multi-stage ultra-marathon in a desert environment. It represents a collection of ideas, research and lessons learned from personal experience to use to help you successfully complete the Marathon des Sables. The guidance contained in the following pages represents the lessons I have learned from failing to complete the race in 2014 and then subsequently returning to successfully complete it the following year.

Please consider this information as a well-educated starting point for your preparation, rather than a guarantee of success. It may be that you are a competitor rather than a 'completer', in which case your training strategy will be entirely different to that laid out in this book. In the event that you are looking to compete with a specific ranking, this guide can still help you, although you will need to supplement it with additional training plans. I would thoroughly recommend that you take a look at the blog post that Danny Kendall wrote in relation to his training. The details of the blog are listed in the Resources chapter of this book.

Book Structure

I wanted to write the type of book that I needed to read, but did not exist when I first attempted the race.

This book covers every single aspect of preparing for the Marathon des Sables, from specific details on kit, nutrition and hydration, to what to carry and wear. This information is broken down into specific chapters, thereby making the book a quick and easy reference guide, which you can dip into as required.

How to Use this Book

I recommend that you skim read the entire book, initially. This will give you a sense of the scale of the commitment you have made, or are intending to make. Thereafter, you should use this book as a reference guide and check back to relevant sections throughout your training, as they become applicable.

Finally, I wish you the very best of luck in your efforts to conquer the toughest footrace on earth.

CHAPTER 3

THE MARATHON DES SABLES

The Toughest Foot Race on Earth

The Marathon des Sables is a gruelling 156-mile, multi-stage ultra-marathon, through what is widely acknowledged to be one of the world's most inhospitable climates: the Sahara Desert.

The race is comprised of six stages split into days, which vary in terms of the distance that must be traversed. The longest stage is 50 miles and must be completed within 34 hours. The race lasts for six days, starting on Saturday and finishing on the following Friday. However, the formal event finishes the day after, which is usually a Saturday, once you have already been awarded your medal.

The rules require you to be self-sufficient. This means carrying everything except water for your own survival, including seven days' worth of food, your own medical kit, "sleep system" and lifesaving emergency equipment, such as an anti-venom pump. Your rucksack weight must be at least 6.5kg without water, but is likely to be quite a bit more.

The race regularly attracts personnel from the armed forces and it is the only race in the world that includes a repatriation fee in the event of death, so that your body can be brought back to your country of origin.

The Marathon des Sables is not for the faint-hearted. Correct preparation and self-management is critical for successful completion of the race. In 2015 alone, one person had a broken ankle, another had two broken toes and two people suffered from broken legs. One woman suffered a ruptured intestine and had to be flown back to the UK for emergency treatment, whilst another experienced temporary blindness caused by low blood sugar levels. One man faced such a severe foot infection that he had to abort the race at 100 miles. In the words of another runner, *"his feet looked like hamburger meat."*

If you don't know anything about the Marathon des Sables and you are looking to do something that is a testament to your mental and physical strength, this is absolutely the race for you. More than a race, the Marathon des Sables is a true statement of your character.

If you have been confirmed entry for the race, congratulations! You have an exciting challenge ahead of you. Unless you have run the race before, it is highly unlikely that you know exactly how to prepare for the extreme challenge that lies ahead of you. Rest assured, you have come to the right place. This book will provide you with all of the information that you are going to need.

I believe that anybody - literally anybody, can run the MdS with the appropriate knowledge and training.

Whether you have already registered for the race and have been confirmed entry, or are mulling it over, the single biggest challenge you will face as a new competitor is preparing for the unknown.

What is the Real Challenge?

Preparing to run the Marathon des Sables is extremely challenging and should be taken very seriously. The race stages vary in terms of length and time limit, but in 2014, they looked like this:

- Stage 1 (Day 1) = 21.1m/ 34km (10 hour time limit)
- Stage 2 (Day 2) = 25.4m/ 41km (11hour time limit)
- Stage 3 (Day 3) = 23.5m/ 37.5km (10.5 hour time limit)
- Stage 4 & 5 (Days 4 & 5) = 50.6m/ 81.5km (34 hour time limit)
- Stage 6 (Day 6) = 26.2m/ 42.4lm (12 hour time limit)

There are many other, additional factors to consider aside from the actual running. Each of these factors will raise many, many more questions. For most first-timers, the questioning, self-doubt and second-guessing continue for the entire duration of your training. Some factors to consider include:

Temperature
The heat in the desert can reach up to 56°C during the day. How is that likely to impact your ability to run on unfamiliar terrain, and how can its effects on the body be managed? Conversely, the temperature in the Sahara can drop to -2°C at night. How will that affect the type of additional kit that you will have to carry in order to manage the cold?

Environment and Terrain
The Sahara landscape includes wadis, the Arabic term for a valley or dry riverbed; jebels, which are essentially mountains or a range of hills; dunes, which are hills or mountains made of sand; and dunettes, which are smaller sand dunes. Many of us don't even know what these look like. What types of training are required and how should that be reflected in terms of overall race strategy?

Multi-Stage Racing
A multi-stage race such as the MdS requires a very different approach from that of a marathon. What sort of self-monitoring and self-management is needed to ensure successful completion of one stage and sufficient preparedness for the next?

Self-Sufficiency and Survival Skills
How does self-sufficiency in relation to nutrition, hydration, navigation, injury management and food preparation during the race translate in the desert?

Rucksack Contents and Kit
How do you decide what should be carried and what you can go without for a multi-stage event? Which shoes, gaiters, clothing and sleep equipment is best?

Race Logistics and Strategy
Given all of the unknowns, how do you decide on a race strategy that combines the appropriate pace, fuel and hydration for the terrain, heat and distance of any one particular stage of the race?

Although there is plenty of information available on the web, in the form of blogs for example, this information is not consolidated, can be conflicting and has not always been validated with the benefit of a runner's hindsight. If you know someone who has run the Marathon des Sables, you will also realise that they are often reluctant to go into the details of what they did, how they did it and why. From experience, I attribute this to the psychological trauma of running such an extreme challenge. From my own research, I found that many MdS runners need significant time to digest what they have been through, which makes re-visiting aspects of MdS training and preparation too difficult, quite simply because that part of the brain had shut down as a coping mechanism. This is unfortunate for an MdS 'newbie', who is typically desperate to learn as much as possible, so that his or her own preparation is as informed as possible.

This book has been written in recognition of these aforementioned difficulties and the awareness of the need for a simple and proven guide to alleviate the anxiety associated MdS preparation. This means that you can stop worrying about the unknown, develop an informed race strategy and give yourself a significant edge in terms of your preparation.

Race Rules and Regulations

There is little point in my listing all the rules and regulations of the race here, since they may become out of date at any point. I urge you strongly to refer to the MdS site (see the Resources chapter for details) for the most current and up-to-date version of the race rules and regulations for your year of race entry.

Types of Entrants

It is useful for you to have an idea of the type of people that enter the Marathon des Sables, because if you are new to ultra-running, you almost definitely doubt whether you have the ability to complete the race. You may even question whether this type of challenge is for you.

In total, the race attracts around 1,300 participants from 43 different countries each year, with around 25% of the runners coming from the UK. A large proportion of entrants are from the military and armed forces and women represent approximately 14% of overall entrants.

30% of those who run are repeat competitors. In other words, they have done it before and came back for more. 10% of competitors walk, whilst 90% alternate between walking and running: 30% of those that enter the MdS do so as part of a team. When I ran the race in 2014 and again in 2015, on both occasions there were blind runners accompanied by support guides. There were people running in their seventies and even eighties. There were also a number of couples. In fact, 2015 even saw its first proposal at the finish line!

From my own personal observations of the 29th and 30th editions of the Marathon des Sables (2014 and 2015, respectively), I can confirm that there is indeed a wide variety and mix of people who run the MdS. You do not need to be an elite runner. In fact, I met a number of people who had not even run a marathon until they started training for the MdS.

Although the race draws a high proportion of military personnel, it also attracts people from different backgrounds, such as professional footballers, rugby players, TV presenters and actors. One of the most famous people to have run the race in 2015 was Sir Ranulph Fiennes, often described as one of the greatest explorers of the twentieth century. Sir Ranulph became the oldest Briton to cross the finish line.

Figure 1: With Sir Ranulph Fiennes, a day before the start of MdS 2015

Irrespective of whether you are single, married, blind, an international explorer, newbie runner, 'too skinny' or 'too fat' – you can definitely complete the Marathon des Sables. The more pertinent question is whether you are ready for what this race entails.

Test Your Readiness

The following questions will determine whether you are in a good place to run the MdS:

1. Does your lifestyle (family, relationship, work, etc.) support your need to train 30-50 miles a week and will it allow you to sustain this for the best part of a year?
2. Are you able to 'rough it' in a tent full of complete strangers, without any privacy and minimal toilet facilities?
3. Are you able to be self-sufficient (e.g. lancing your own blisters, navigating your route, ensuring appropriate nutrition and hydration)?
4. Can you manage not showering and living in the same clothes for a whole week?
5. Are you prepared to carry up to 10kg on your back while running or walking, across the desert for an entire week?
6. Would you be able to cope with managing injuries, such as lost toenails, whilst training for the race or during the race itself?
7. If you are doing the race with someone, could you cope if they dropped out or got injured, leaving you run alone?
8. Can you cope with long stretches of being alone during the day and potentially through the night?
9. Can you lift your own mood easily in times of stress?
10. Do you have a comprehensive list of reasons why you *have* to do this race?

If you answered, "yes" to five or more of these questions, you are in a good place to run the MdS. I recommend coming back to these questions during your training, to reassure yourself of how mentally strong you already are and continue to become, as a result of all of your hard work. If you cannot answer, "yes" to at least five of these questions, I would seriously reconsider embarking on this endeavour in the immediate future.

Question 10 is particularly important, because training for the MdS requires a vast amount of personal strength. As your training intensifies, you will keep coming back to the same question: "Why am I putting myself through this?" For this reason, you will need some very definite answers.

Registering for the Marathon des Sables

If you have yet to register for the Marathon des Sables, you will soon realise that securing a place for this race is no easy feat; the competition is fierce and there are many more applicants than places.

UK entry must be made through the official UK site, although if you have dual nationality you can enter through an alternative country's official site, instead (see the Resources chapter for details). This approach may be a more cost-effective method, because entry prices vary from country to country.

Once on the site, select the registration button and choose the year you are interested in. You will be prompted to complete a sign-up box, which means that you will be notified when the registration process is "live". You will need to pay a £500 fee when you register.

Registration for the race takes place in June of each year and you need to be very quick and organised about securing a place, because places literally disappear within minutes. You will need your payment details and passport number. Expect the site to be slow due to the number of people trying to register at the same time. In the event that all the places have been filled, you will be invited to join the waiting list but will still need to pay the £500 deposit. Don't panic if this happens. If you are high on the list, you are virtually guaranteed a place because so many people drop out due to injury, unexpected commitments and even through fear.

You will receive a confirmation email once your registration is successful and at this point, your journey begins.

CHAPTER 4

TRAINING STRATEGY

This chapter covers the physical and mental training that I used to successfully complete the Marathon des Sables. The contents are based on my own personal experiences of successfully completing the race and the lessons that I learned from failing to complete at first attempt.

Realities of the Race

We have already learned that the MdS is a multi-stage ultra-marathon and that the temperature can be as extreme as 56°C in the daytime and -2°C at night. The terrain is extremely varied; only 20% of the desert is comprised of sand.

As you also know, the race requires you to be completely self-sufficient; you must be able to carry your entire equipment and all supplies - including food, sleeping bag and medical equipment, on your back for the entire duration of the race. You must be able to 'rough it', which means wearing the same clothes for seven days, not being able to shower and having the most basic of toilet facilities. You must be able to camp in a tent with men and women. You must have mental toughness and resilience to push through moments of extreme pain and loneliness and you absolutely need to have a positive spirit; not only to successfully finish race, but also to get you through the extreme demands required by training for such an event.

4 Things You MUST Be Able to Do

My experiences of the Marathon des Sables in 2014 and 2015 have taught me that, irrespective of whether your goal is to complete or compete in the race, an effective training programme must be designed in such a way that it:

- allows you to run at least 20 miles, walking when you have to;
- with your MdS rucksack, which contains the anticipated weight of your actual equipment;
- across varied and undulating terrain;
- over a number of consecutive days.

Achieving such a huge goal will require a significant amount of training, which must be built up very slowly over time to avoid injuries. As I progressed through my training programme, I found that these goals became more and more achievable because I had trained specifically to achieve them.

On top of this, it is important to:

- remain injury free as far as possible during your training
- manage any injuries you develop during your training

- manage yourself constantly during the race in terms of fuel and hydration
- take responsibility for your own medical and foot care requirements before, during and after the race
- 'rough it' and cope with extreme changes of temperature
- remain conscious of your pace and be able to adjust it relative to the stipulated time limits.

If you can successfully do these, you have every chance of completing the Marathon des Sables.

The first time that I attempted MdS, I developed a number of injuries during my training, including: severe plantar fasciitis; many, many blisters; as many as eight lost toenails; and iliotibial band syndrome - all of which are discussed later in this book. The list of injuries just went on and on, leaving me in a permanent state of anxiety. The second time I trained for MdS, I was injury-free during my training, despite the fact that I was running far greater distances with full pack weight for at least 4 months before the race. At my training peak, I was running 100 miles in one week whilst carrying 10kg on my small 5"1 frame. During the race, I developed blisters, but these were well-managed and caused me few problems during or after the race.

I attribute my lack of injuries to two key factors. Firstly, I developed and followed a graduated training programme. This meant that the distance that I covered, along with the weight that I carried during my training, was increased slowly and incrementally. During and after each training run, I would pay attention to how my body felt; if there was a twinge or an unfamiliar pain, I would monitor it and take a day off if I needed to. In hindsight, this cycle of noticing, responding and adjusting paid dividends, because it prevented me from overdoing training and suffering injuries unnecessarily. Secondly, during my training, I tried and tested absolutely everything that I intended to use, consume or wear in the desert. I did this trial and testing as soon as possible and as frequently as possible in training, with the intention of minimising any surprises during what I already knew to be stressful circumstances.

Running or Walking?

The reality of the heat and terrain of the MdS means that many people will end up walking significant parts of the race. However, since most people have commitments such as family and work outside of training for the MdS, going for 20-mile training hikes for hours and hours on a regular basis is simply not an option.

If you are intending to walk for the whole duration of the race, have absolutely no desire or intention to run whatsoever and have the time to commit to a training plan that consists entirely of walking, you can absolutely do that. If you are easily able to sustain a 15 minute mile pace or less over undulating terrain, you would make a suitable candidate for walking MdS, provided that you can also deal with all of the other elements of the race, such as heat, rucksack weight, etc.

Personally, I advocate against a walking-only training approach, based on my own bitter experience. The first time we did MdS, my friend Simon and I were intending to walk the entire race. However, the mixed and often severe terrain, combined with the heat and the weight of our rucksack made our average pace very, very slow. We arrived back at camp very late and the later we arrived, the less time we had for recovery and preparation for the next day. This meant that each day became progressively more difficult than it needed to be.

Figure 2 considers a number of elements based on your personal race ambitions. The left-hand column identifies elements such as MdS pace, the time you can expect to spend running or walking between checkpoints, the total time you are likely to be on your feet, along with the expected recovery time over the duration of the race. You will notice that the differences between the two are somewhat significant and depend on whether your ambition is to compete, i.e. gain a top 10 position, or to simply complete the race.

	Race Aspirations	
	To compete (i.e. gain a top 10 spot)	To complete (i.e. just finish)
MdS pace	11.5km/h (mostly running)	3.5km/h (mostly walking)
Run/ walk time Between check points	Approx. 1 hour	Approx. 3 hours
Time on feet	Approx. 21 hours	Approx. 70 hours
Available recovery time during race	More than 120 hours	Less than 75 hours

Figure 2: Comparison between different race aspirations

Since the MdS is a multi-stage event, I'm personally in favour of running as much of it as you possibly can, so that you have the maximum opportunity to rest and recover, in preparation for the next stage.

Additionally, it is important to get as many miles into your training as possible, since this will help to condition your feet for the huge distances you will have to cover. It also means that your whole physiology, including your core and back muscles, will be conditioned not only to run great distances, but also to carry the required weight over those distances.

Compete or Complete

The previous table illustrated how different elements of the race, such as pace, overall running or walking times between check points, time on feet and recovery time might look depending on your personal aspirations. These findings only consider two extremes on the spectrum of aspirations and depend on whether you hope to achieve a top 10 position or simply to complete the race.

Figure 3 illustrates what a daily schedule may look like depending on an individual's aspirations. The schedule identifies three types of competitor: fast-paced runners who use a run-only strategy, medium-paced or 'middle of the pack' runners who use a run/walk strategy and those that are much slower-paced and predominantly walk.

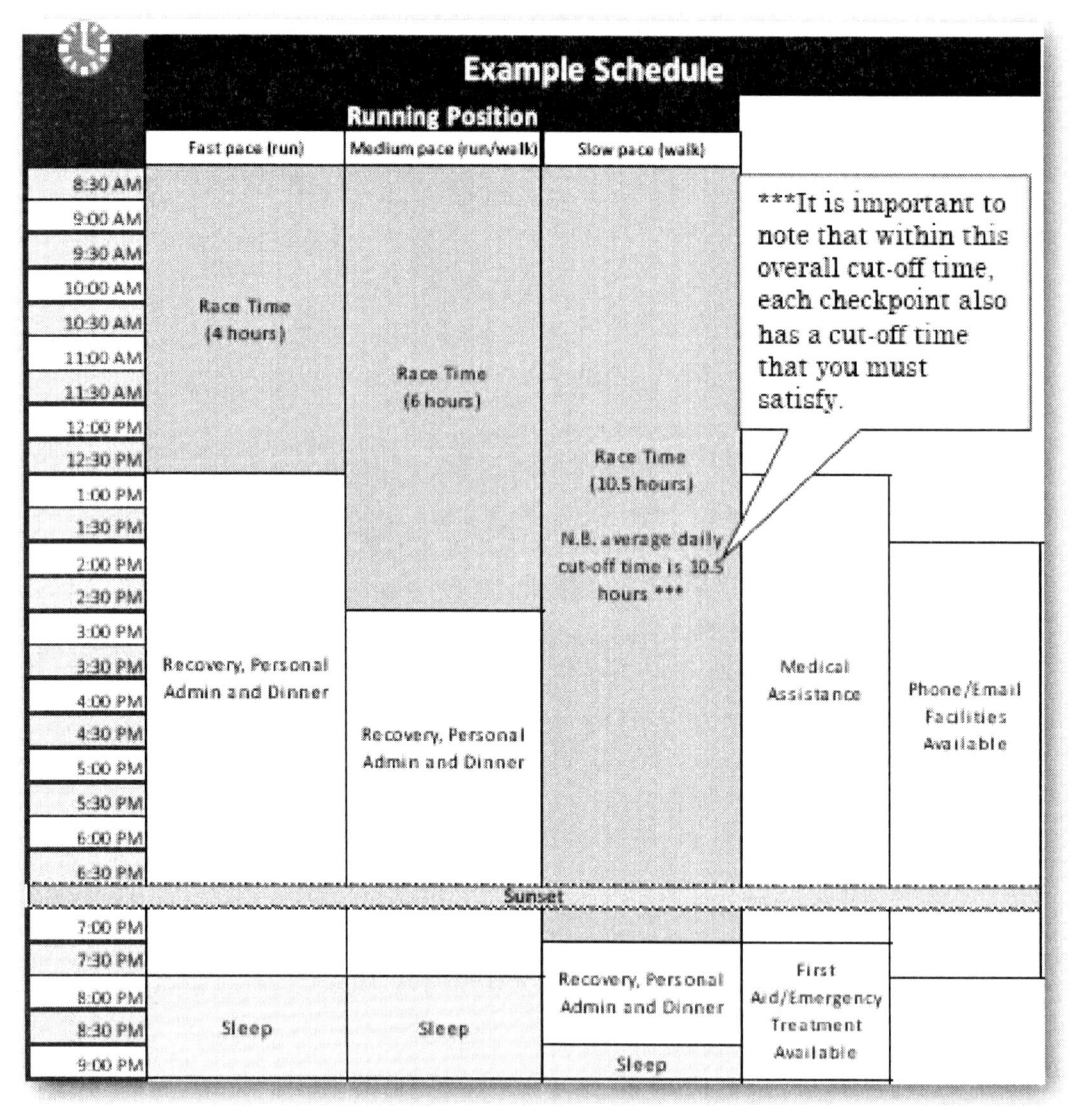

Time	Fast pace (run)	Medium pace (run/walk)	Slow pace (walk)		
8:30 AM – 12:30 PM	Race Time (4 hours)	Race Time (6 hours)	Race Time (10.5 hours) N.B. average daily cut-off time is 10.5 hours ***		***It is important to note that within this overall cut-off time, each checkpoint also has a cut-off time that you must satisfy.
1:00 PM – 3:00 PM	Recovery, Personal Admin and Dinner			Medical Assistance	Phone/Email Facilities Available
3:30 PM – 6:30 PM		Recovery, Personal Admin and Dinner			
Sunset					
7:00 PM – 9:00 PM	Sleep	Sleep	Recovery, Personal Admin and Dinner / Sleep	First Aid/Emergency Treatment Available	

Figure 3: Example schedule depending on race strategy

Figure 3 shows that those who spend a significant proportion of their day on their feet (denoted as, "Race Time"), have much shorter time for personal administration (e.g. foot care, washing, dinner and reading messages from home). Figure 3 also shows that slow runners and walkers have a later bed time and shorter sleep period. Ultimately, these factors translate into less time for the body to optimally recover for the next day.

This information may seem trivial to the uninitiated, but given the cumulative mental and physical tiredness over 6 solid days of running, it becomes significant. Failure to realise this may be hugely detrimental to your race experience, as it was for me in 2014. For such reasons, this information should absolutely inform your race strategy, and therefore your training plan.

MdS Training Principles

The following training principles are derived from my own training plan:

1. **Focus predominantly on running rather than walking**, although walking intermittently when necessary is fine.

2. **Increase mileage incrementally.** In the same way that training programmes for marathons advise a 10% increase in distance for long runs, ultra-distances must also be subject to the same sort of cautious increase in mileage to minimise the likelihood of injury.

3. **Add weight gradually** and only once you can comfortably run 10 miles at a slow and steady pace.

4. **Train with a rucksack that contains your actual kit**:
   - This forces you to be organised and not delay kit testing and purchasing unnecessarily.
   - Any discomfort from weight distribution or actual kit will be experienced early, allowing you to make any adjustments as soon as possible.
   - The contents of your rucksack will sit on your back differently to other types of weights, such as bags of salt. However, you could use bags of salt as an interim measure if you are in the process of buying kit. Many supermarkets sell 1kg packets of salt, which make incremental addition of weight much easier.
   - You will learn to hydrate as you run and fuel using the actual food items you intend to take with you for the race.
   - You will be forced to think about where to put items that need to be within easy reach, such as toilet roll, hand sanitiser, compass, road book.

5. **Hike on hilly terrain carrying the weight of your rucksack.** A lot of the Marathon des Sables involves walking over undulating, rocky or mountainous terrain. You must be very comfortable walking at a sustained pace with your rucksack weight, irrespective of terrain.

6. **Include milestones that simulate race conditions in your training plan.** My training, for example, included back-to-back 20 mile runs, carrying my actual rucksack at anticipated weight and 50 mile runs to replicate the long stage of the race.

7. **Include strength-building exercises in your training plan.** Having a strong core, quadriceps and calves will give you the physical strength you will need in order to deal with the demands of the race, but will also help prevent injuries.

8. **Factor psychological training into the plan by understanding how you react to discomfort.** This is important because it will help you manage your mental health when you are in extreme discomfort. How will you talk yourself out of negative thinking at specific points in the race? How will you gain a sense of perspective when the heat of the day hits you and you are physically and mentally exhausted? My own method for dealing with such exhaustion is described under the Mental Strength Training section of this chapter.

Comparison Between 2014 and 2015 Race Strategies

Figure 4 illustrates the differences in my race strategies for the Marathon des Sables in 2014, when I failed to complete, and in 2015, when I completed the race successfully.

Figure 4 shows differences in terms of race result, training experience, average and peak weekly mileage, % of runs with a rucksack, method and amount of training for heat acclimatisation, rucksack weight and the extent to which my social life was impacted as I trained for the race.

	Year of Race	
	2014	**2015**
Result	Failed at 3rd stage	Completed
Training style	Significant marathon experience; no sand/ trail/ cross country running	Extensive hiking; hill, sand and cross-country running; MdS specific training
Average weekly mileage	30-35 miles	50-55 miles
Peak weekly mileage	50 miles	100 miles
Training with rucksack	Less that 10% of all runs	January - March, 100% of runs (gradual increase of 0.5kg, every two weeks)
Rucksack weight (with water)	14kg	8kg
Heat acclimitisation	Bikram Yoga over 3 months	Sauna - 10 hours, 1 week beforehand
Social life	Busy	Less than 75 hours

Figure 4: Comparison between my race strategies

A Graduated Training Programme

As discussed, your training programme should be based on a plan enabling you to run at least 20 miles consistently, walking when you have to, whilst carrying the anticipated weight and actual equipment in your race rucksack, across varied and undulating terrain, over a number of consecutive days.

Reaching Marathon Distance

I built up to marathon distance in a safe, gradual way before moving onto ultra-marathon distances. I followed a basic 16-week training plan, which focused on distance rather than speed. After the 16-week period, your training plan can begin to transition from a marathon-training plan into an ultra-marathon plan, suitable for the MdS.

16 week Marathon Training Plan

Figure 5 shows the basic training plan I followed. This marathon plan is designed for the novice runner, intending to complete a first marathon. You can see that the mileage increases incrementally.

By spreading the mileage throughout the week and the long run on the weekend, you'll stay healthy and have enough training under your belt to reach marathon distance. All slow runs should be run at an easy, conversational pace.

Week	Mon	Tue	Wed	Thu	Fri	Sat	Sun	Total Mileage
1	3	REST	4	3	REST	5	REST	15
2	3	REST	4	3	REST	6	REST	16
3	3	REST	4	3	REST	7	REST	17
4	3	REST	5	3	REST	8	REST	19
5	3	REST	5	3	REST	10	REST	21
6	4	REST	5	4	REST	11	REST	24
7	4	REST	6	4	REST	12	REST	26
8	4	REST	6	4	REST	14	REST	28
9	4	REST	7	4	REST	16	REST	31
10	5	REST	8	4	REST	16	REST	33
11	5	REST	8	5	REST	18	REST	36
12	5	REST	8	5	REST	18	REST	36
13	5	REST	8	5	REST	20	REST	38
14	5	REST	8	5	REST	9	REST	27
15	3	REST	5	3	REST	8	REST	19
16	3	REST	3	2	REST	26.2	REST	34.2

Figure 5: Example 16 week marathon training plan

As someone intending to run the MdS, it goes without saying that you need to get used to running on a regular basis. For this reason, the plan I used incorporated four days of running and three days of complete or 'active' rest.

Active rest, sometimes referred to as active recovery, is defined as very light exercise other than running and often includes stretching to avoid damaging overworked muscles. This may also include swimming or taking a yoga class the day after a tough workout.

Some Training Plan Considerations

- Each run should have a specific *purpose*. This means that you should not be running at the same pace every time you train, to ensure that your fitness does not plateau too quickly. During my training, I tried to incorporate easy runs, intervals, hills training, both long and slow runs, and "recovery" runs. Please note that this is not reflected in Figure 5, which is a training plan that demonstrates the split of mileage per day and over a series of weeks. For clarification, your training may include the following types of run:
    - **Easy runs,** which involve a continuous and sustained run at a pace. The easy run is executed in a relaxed way with little conscious control.
    - **Intervals** are short, intense efforts followed by equal or slightly longer recovery time. For example, after a warm-up, run two minutes at a hard effort, followed by two to three minutes of easy jogging or walking to catch your breath. Unlike tempo workouts, where you're

running at an effort that requires you to reach hard for air and where you are counting the seconds until you can stop, intervals demand a controlled fast effort followed by a truly easy jog. Each interval should be sustainable.
- **Tempo runs** refer to the effort level just outside your comfort zone, where you can hear your breathing, but you're not gasping for air. If you can talk easily, you're not in the tempo zone, and if you can't talk at all, you're above the zone. It should be at an effort somewhere in the middle, so you can talk in broken words.
- **Hill training** can come in many forms. These include continuous running across hilly terrain, short hill intervals, long hill intervals, tempo hill training and treadmill hill running.
- **Speed training.** This is more relevant for the MdS if you have ambitious goals in terms of competing for a position. However, even if you only want to finish and plan to walk most of the event, speed work will still help your overall fitness, as will interval training and tempo running.

- You might want to consider scheduling in a marathon once you are able to run 20 miles comfortably. Since you are putting so much into training, it makes sense to get used to race conditions, albeit different race conditions. The Resources chapter of this book will give you an indication of the types of races that will help prepare you specifically for MdS to ensure that you remain on track with your end goal.
- Your rucksack should be the actual rucksack you will be taking with you to the desert. I cannot stress this enough. I met a lot of runners who trained with a completely different rucksack and then, during the race, suffered tremendous chafing and discomfort.
- You should add weight to your long runs by carrying the *actual* equipment and supplies you intend to be using for MdS - although it may take time for you to test and buy all of the equipment that is appropriate for you. In this case, you should use bags of salt or 0.5 litre bottles of water and replace these with your actual kit as soon as is practical for you. Note that the actual kit will sit against your back and will feel very different to salt bags or water bottles.
- Use your long runs as opportunities to test out the snacks you might want to eat in the desert. For a traditional marathon, many runners use gels, but these can be sickly in the heat of the Sahara. You can find more ideas for nutrition while running, in the Food and Hydration chapter of this book.
- Try to avoid training purely on pavement and aim to include trail runs during training. These will help to strengthen your joints and tendons and therefore help prevent any injuries.
- Listen to your body and mind. You will have a number of months to go after you have reached the initial objective of marathon level fitness, which means that it is important for you not to burn out or injure yourself. If you need a week or two off to maintain overall mental and physical focus, you should take it.
- Include a tapering strategy. This means ensuring ample time to build energy reserves and to rest your body before the actual race. My tapering plan for the MdS was only two weeks. I reduced the mileage I was running, but maintained the effort. In my opinion, this is a cost versus benefits argument, after all, realistically how much will you increase fitness in the final four weeks before a race? You will, however, significantly increase your risk of injury by continuing to push too hard.

Alternative Training Plans

Your decision to use a traditional, graduated marathon training plan will depend on a number of factors. You may not have the time to follow a suggested 16-week plan; you may find it too easy or you may already be at marathon level fitness with your own tried and tested training plan.

For practical reasons, it is not feasible to include every single training plan option within the confines of this book. There are plenty of online resources that will meet your requirements and as long as you reach the initial objective of being able to run a marathon comfortably, the type of plan is irrelevant. I recommend Runner's World as a great initial resource if you are looking for training plan alternatives.

Performance Implications

While developing a training strategy for MdS, it is worth considering the likely performance implications of specific aspects of your training. Your weekly training distances, the length of your long runs and the frequency with which you train will all have an impact on your overall MdS performance, so it makes sense to become informed regarding these factors before you develop your own training strategy.

Weekly Training Distance and Performance

Research conducted by ultra-runner and MdS veteran Genis Pieterse, found that there is a direct correlation between weekly distances covered and race performance. Following his studies from the 2013 Marathon des Sables, Pieterse found that a manageable training program derived from the MdS research data would consist of the following average weekly distances:

Participant type	Weeks 12-8	Weeks 8-4	Weeks 4-0
Competitive Runner (Top 10%)	85km/ 53m	90km/ 56m	80km/ 50m
Casual Runner (majority of participants)	70km/ 44m	70km/ 43m	60km/ 37m
Aim to just complete (bottom 10%)	55km/ 34m	55km/ 34m	50km/ 31m

Figure 6: Relationship between weekly distance and performance in the countdown to the race
(Source: www.Push2Extreme.com, Genis Pieterse)

From Figure 6, we can see that, at an absolute minimum, you must be able to run up to 35 miles per week consistently during your training and definitely in the last three months before the race. If you are looking to achieve the same sorts of results as the majority of runners, you will need to increase your mileage to almost 45 miles. Furthermore, a desire to compete for a highly-ranked position means that your average weekly mileage must be at least 50 miles a week in the last three months preceding participation in the MdS.

The Role of a Long Run and Impact on Performance

Figure 7 describes the relationship between the frequency of long runs during training and the corresponding impact on race performance.

Position	Long runs over 12 weeks (Distance & frequency)	Average long run distance
Top 10%	12 (one per week)	31km/ 19m
Next 20%	8 (two every 3 weeks)	28km/ 17m
Next 40%	6 (one every 2 weeks)	29m/ 18m
Next 20%	8 (two every 3 weeks)	25km/ 16m
Bottom 10%	4 (one per month)	30km/ 19m

Figure 7: Relationship between long run frequency and MdS race position
(Source: www.Push2Extreme.com, Genis Pieterse)

The average distance of a long run is relatively similar across all performance groups. However, the *frequency* of these runs is where we see a significant difference. Whilst both the top and bottom 10% of performers run an average long-run distance of 30km/ 19m, the top 10% does so once a week while the bottom 10% does so only once a month.

This indicates that the more frequent your long runs are, the better your race performance is likely to be.

Finding Appropriate Terrain

Whilst in training for the 2015 MdS, I incorporated long, hilly hikes into my training programme, which would often replace my long, slow runs. This is because, for the vast number of MdS participants, walking makes up a large portion of the race. On the face of it, this might sound easy, but when the distance and the heat are accompanied by a heavy rucksack and difficult terrain, staying within the checkpoint time limits can become a tough challenge. Walking will also mean that you have less time to recover after each stage, as discussed earlier in this chapter. For this reason, I would propose using long, hilly hikes as a means of building back and leg strength. Where you can, you should try to jog or 'shuffle', since this is a more realistic scenario for most people.

The South Downs Way is a very popular training ground for those doing the MdS. It is very accessible for those who live in and around London and the muddy terrain during the Winter and Spring months provide a reasonably good simulation of the desert's sandy conditions.

You may want to incorporate some specific hikes into your training for the MdS. If, like me, you are UK based, I recommend:

- 7 Sisters & Beachy Head, Eastbourne to Seaford (13 miles)
- Amberley to Lewes, South Downs Way (28.5 miles)
- Lewes to Berwick, South Downs Way (16 miles)
- Box Hill and surrounding area (approx. 12 miles)
- The Jurassic Coast (approx. 25 miles)

I used a run/walk strategy for these hikes and repeated them several times over the course of my training schedule, since the terrain was appropriately strenuous and the routes were relatively straightforward.

Training Groups

You can do your running training alone or you can find other MdS runners to train with, who might live locally. The best way to do this is via the MdS Facebook group, the details of which are contained in the Resources chapter, under General Information. You can also find support via local running groups and through friends who may want to do some races with you.

Generally, training for the MdS can be a horribly lonely and isolating experience. I strongly recommend joining a hiking group; it will allow you build an even bigger network of friends who can help and support you during your tough training regime. From a solo female perspective, this is also a lot safer.

Unfortunately, some runners can be quite snobbish about hikers, because they view hiking as a 'soft' option. However, if you consider that some of those hikers are capable of maintaining a consistent speed of around 4 miles an hour over undulating and extremely hilly terrain, you will realise that there is actually quite a lot of skill to walking very fast!

As previously mentioned, incorporating long hikes over undulating terrain will test and develop your ability to carry your rucksack over long periods of time. This will help to toughen up your feet and train various muscle groups, including your core and gluteal muscles, and it will prepare you physically and mentally for the realities of the Marathon des Sables. Finally, it will also give you a great opportunity to test out specific kit, such as walking poles, which you cannot do on pavement.

I hiked distances of 20+ miles every 2-3 weeks in the 4-5 months prior to MdS. This was to break up the monotony of running for many months, but also to get used to walking and running with my full pack weight where possible, so my body would be appropriately conditioned for the race.

I joined hiking groups that specialised in fast, hilly hikes via an organisation called Meet Up. Some of these groups charge a small fee per hike, whilst others do not. In all cases, you pay for your own transport and other costs.

More often than not, I would take my full MdS kit, along with Raidlight water bottles and run sections of the hike. There is no way that you can join such a group incognito, because you will stand out like a sore thumb. I would recommend being upfront and explaining why you have joined the group and what you want to gain from membership. I found that when I did this, I had great support from everyone I ever hiked with. Details of Meet Up can be found in the Resources chapter of this book.

Milestone Races and Hikes

There are a number of milestone races and hikes that MdS runners tend to participate in, such as the Druids Challenge and the Pilgrims Challenge. These races are listed in the Resources chapter, under Training Races and are especially useful for MdS runners because they simulate the varied terrain and the multi-day aspect of MdS.

These milestones will allow you to start building up your ultra-distances. I recommend incorporating a number of 20-30 mile hikes into your training plan once you can run 20 miles, since your joints will now be used to long distances.

Multi-Stage Events

Multi-stage events are incredibly useful in your preparation for MdS. Your hiking activities, combined with your ability to run long distances with weight, will put you in a very good position to be able to complete and even compete in such events. Although I was unable to participate in the formal Druids Challenge or the Pilgrims Challenge, I did organise my own hikes with some friends, following the same routes in similar conditions.

My training plan also incorporated a 'mini' MdS. Specifically, this involved running 20 miles every day for five consecutive days, with my fully-packed rucksack. This was at the peak of my MdS training, when I was running 100 miles in one week at a pace of between 4mph-5mph. I walked where I needed to, but ran around 90% of the distance. I found this to be excellent preparation for the MdS, because it was a close simulation of the distances that would be covered, complete with the actual kit weight on my back. I wanted to test the way my mind and physiology would respond to covering such distances back-to-back over a five-day period.

The longest stage of MdS is the 50-mile stage, although in 2015 this was increased to almost 60 miles in 'celebration' of the 30th Anniversary. I included two separate 50 mile runs as additional milestones within my training and approached each one as two 25 milers, with a 2.5-hour break in between each stage.

I found that because I had built up my training incrementally, my recovery time was very quick. I would definitely recommend taking protein and carbohydrate powders to aid your post-run recovery. My personal preference is SIS Rego Rapid Recovery powder consumed within 20 minutes of a long run.

Cross-Training

I would recommend regular strength training for specific muscle groups, such as core, back, quadriceps, gluteal and calf muscles. The first time I did MdS, I had done literally no calf training and really, really felt the strain, particularly ascending and descending the steep jebels and dunes. Whilst cross-fit can offer great strength-building exercises, unless you have already been used to training in this way for some time, I would be inclined to stay away from it due to the potential for unnecessary injury during this type of training.

Although cross-training will not necessarily improve a runner's performance as much as additional running would, anything that helps with weight loss and builds muscle and cardiovascular fitness is a positive. It's important to prioritise workouts that give the biggest benefit. I knew that I had weak back muscles, calves and hip flexors, so focused my strength training on these specific areas.

Given that many of us have jobs, families and social lives, it makes sense to do the training that is most applicable and provides the greatest return on investment in terms of time, effort and money.

Sand Training

I found it useful to train on sand a few times, to get an idea of what it would feel like underfoot, but also to understand how my running style would need to adapt to the different terrain. There are a number of places you can go in the UK to try sand dune training including Camber Sands and Southport. The best place to go, if you have the resources, is the Dune du Pilat in Bordeaux, which is home to the highest sand dune in Europe. If you are going to make this trip, I would advise you to try and replicate the conditions that you will experience during the race as closely as possible. This means having your trainers with gaiters already attached; your rucksack with the anticipated weight you will be carrying for the week, and walking poles, to test them out.

Your strategy for navigating different terrain during the MdS will vary. For example, there is no point trying to run up vertical sand dunes, because it makes more sense to look for the footprints of previous runners to make climbing the sand dunes easier. When coming down the huge sand dunes, try to allow yourself to fall forward so that your body is able to lead from the hips. This will enable you to use your body weight to create speed and momentum, thereby utilising gravity to make the decline with minimal exertion.

Mental Strength Training

The nature of training for MdS is so all-consuming that you will become both physically and mentally stronger than you ever were pre-training. You will need immense mental resolve to overcome inertia in order to enable you to train in all types of weather, across all terrain, whilst managing work life, family life and personal hobbies. As challenging as this sounds, there are a number of things you can do to help yourself in achieving this:

During Your Training

If you are in the early stages of a marathon training plan, recognise that the hardest parts are at the beginning and the peak of your training plan. Things will become more 'enjoyable' once you reach double digits (10 miles or more) in your training, because by that point you know that you have the mental strength to just get on and do it.

I have always believed that it takes six weeks to make or break a habit and that during this time my mind will work against me. To that end, I recommend anticipating and preparing for those times when everything is telling you to give up. Acknowledge that you do not feel like going for a run and get ready, anyway. I used to say, *"I really don't want to go because it's raining, but I'll just get changed into my gear in case.... I'll just fill my water bottles, too."* Before I knew it, I was out of the door! Be prepared and put your kit out the night before each training run. I remember in the very hardest times, I would even sleep in my running gear to minimise procrastination in the morning.

Finally, use the resources available to you to the fullest extent. In my experience, friends, family and even colleagues can be vital in supporting you during your training. I would ask one friend to text me to ensure I was actually heading out to do my dreaded long run, as I had intended. Another friend would leave a banana on my desk every Thursday morning as a reward for my pre-work run. During my 50-mile runs for MdS, friends would message me with encouragement while I was running. There are an infinite number of ways that people can help you and you might be surprised how many will be glad to assist and willingly play a part in your success.

As you move past the stage where you can run 20 miles or more, you will need to start wearing your actual MdS kit and rucksack. When you feel self-conscious in MdS gear, make use of the attention in a positive way. I was raising money for Macmillan Cancer Support and reasoned that since people were staring at me anyway, it made sense to use my training runs as an opportunity to advertise my cause. I created an A4 size poster, laminated it and put it on the back of my bag to tell passers-by why I was dressed the way I was and how they could text a specific number to donate to my charitable cause.

To combat lethargy, I recommend varying your training with other exercise, such as swimming, cycling or hiking. You could also try running new routes or listening to audio books while running. The latter worked very well for me as an incentive to go for long, slow runs, detracting from the boredom of those seemingly endless miles.

Be sure to celebrate your milestones. Although your plan might recognise the big milestones as one 20-mile run or back-to-back long runs, a week where you have completed any long run and managed to remain injury free is still plenty of cause for celebration.

Lastly, give yourself a break. There will definitely be times when you are mentally and physically tired and whilst you may not be injured, your emotional wellbeing must be monitored, too. Your personal circumstances may change, thereby making training difficult. In this case, it's okay to take an entire week - or even several weeks off, over a number of months and to adjust your training accordingly. Ignore minor setbacks, because perseverance really is the key to successful training.

During the Race
Your mental strength during the race is critically important. I significantly underestimated the value of this the first time I did MdS and it resulted in my internal dialogue telling me that I could not do it, that I was tired, that it was too hot, that my pack was too heavy and that if I failed, no-one would care.

For my second attempt at MdS, I had a long list of worries. These included a fear of being too slow, loneliness during the long stage, fear of becoming injured and my mind and internal dialogue chattering away so that it worked against me, ultimately resulting in me giving up. It is okay to experience fear. In fact, it is important. However, fear can become irrational and sometimes, even crippling.

There are plenty of NLP (Neuro Linguistic Programming) techniques you can use or develop to deal with your fears. Unfortunately, it is beyond the scope of this book to cover all of these techniques, but I can share one particular technique that I developed for myself, which worked incredibly well in tackling all of the aforementioned fears.

Whenever a negative thought manifested itself during the race, either mentally or through a physical feeling such as tightened neck muscles, a clenched jaw, etc., I imagined that it took the form of a squash ball coming towards me at a great speed and was about to smash me in the face. The second I experienced a "squash ball moment", I mentally visualised using the entire force of my body to smack it with an imaginary squash racquet. Of course, it sounds ridiculous - but if it works, who cares?

Fitting It All In
To say that there is a lot of training involved for the MdS is a huge understatement. Think of marathon training and multiply it by ten, to understand the effort and commitment you need in order to just get through the training. I can reassure you that the panic you are feeling is normal.

Your training plan must take into account what you can realistically commit to, given your lifestyle. You *can* complete the MdS with a 30 mile per week training schedule BUT it will be tough because you will have very long and hard days during the race with minimal time for rest and recovery. The lack of time spent on your feet during training will translate into some foot issues in the desert, but if you are mentally strong and motivated, that medal will hang around your neck at the end of the marathon stage. Any weekly distance over and above this 30 miles per week will make the race progressively more bearable, and in many cases, highly enjoyable. I would recommend using the commute to work as a way of incorporating your training around your schedule. I would often run 5 or 6 miles before work and a further five or six miles after work. My long runs would be left for the weekend, where I could commit a few hours more easily.

At this point, you already know that the huge distance covered during training is no guarantee that you will finish the race. You have to manage yourself in the desert very carefully and constantly monitor your body and mind throughout every stage of the race. The MdS is a test of self-sufficiency as much as a test of training. The factors that are critical to the race, other than training, are considered in the following chapters of this book.

CHAPTER 5

WHAT TO CARRY

This chapter considers what you should take with you for the duration of the race. For ease of reference, other aspects of the race are considered in the subsequent chapters of this book.

It is important to note that at the time of writing, the MdS organisers stipulated that all personal belongings for each competitor, including mandatory equipment, should weigh 6.5kg as a minimum, not including water. This is known as "dry pack weight".

It is extremely important to invest some time into thinking about what you will take with you to the desert. The first time I did MdS, I made substantial errors in terms of packing. There is a far greater risk of over-packing than under-packing. I have read suggestions that if you are a bottom-of-the-pack runner, you should carry extra home comforts to make the race as comfortable as possible for yourself. Personally, I advocate against this. In fact, from experience, I can confirm that this is ridiculous advice. If you over-pack, you will be carrying excess weight for the duration of the race, which, when combined with the heat and terrain of the desert, will make you much slower. This excessive weight will impact your joints and posture, as well as put greater pressure on your whole physiology, including your feet, and thereby increasing the likelihood of blisters and other injuries.

Where possible, try to make the items that you carry fulfil multiple purposes. I will elaborate on this as we progress through the details of the kit list.

This chapter is split into two sections; mandatory equipment and additional kit.

Mandatory Equipment

The following list identifies the mandatory equipment required to run the MdS, and is categorised by whether they are supplied by the organisers of MdS or not.

For those items that are not supplied, the expectation is that you will research and trial equipment during your training, and that you will select items that meet not only your needs, but also fulfil the mandatory kit requirements of the organisation.

It is important to note that this list will be checked on administration day and that any problems in terms of meeting the stipulated requirements may result in race disqualification. For this reason, it is critically important that you review the most recent mandatory kit list that is provided by the organisation.

Mandatory Kit List

Items supplied by the organisation:

- Road book
- GPS device (previously a distress flare)

- Transponder
- Glow stick
- Salt tablets
- Sanitary bags for the toilets
- ID markers

Items not supplied by the organisation:

- Rucksack
- Sleeping bag
- Head torch with spare batteries
- 10 safety pins
- Compass, accurate to 1°-2°
- Lighter (you have to carry this, even if you are not intending to use cooking fuel)
- Whistle
- Knife with metal blade
- Topical disinfectant
- Anti-venom pump
- Signalling mirror
- Aluminium survival sheet
- Sun cream
- 200 Euros

Mandatory Kit – List Review

The following section considers each item identified in the aforementioned list in more detail. It incorporates recommendations based on research and my own personal experience.

Road Book

The road book will be given to you upon arrival in Morocco. Your starting point may or may not be Errachidia. Irrespective of where you land, once out of the airport, you will be waiting in a coach for a number of hours before being taken to the camp. During this time, you will also receive several litres of water and a packed lunch. You should use this time to become familiar with the road book.

When you open the book, you will see that the road book directions are in French first and then in English. I recommend familiarising yourself with the overall race route along with the rules and regulations of the race. I used a bright highlighter pen to highlight the directions that were in English. This is helpful because during the race, when you are tired, it is incredibly difficult to focus on the bits that are important - so highlight them before the race starts. It will also make it a lot easier to skim through the directions on the morning of the next stage. You should pack your highlighter pen away in your suitcase rather than carry it with you during the race. I recommend packing the road book in a place that allows you to access it easily while running.

Glow Stick

The only item not provided before the race begins is the glow stick. In 2015, this was issued at Check Point 3 during the long stage, before night fell. The glow stick should be attached to the back of your rucksack and is designed to ensure your visibility during the long stage. The GPS device and transponder will be taken from you at the end of the charity stage, which is the last formal stage of the race.

Remaining Items

The remaining items will be provided to you a day before the race begins, along with appropriate usage instructions. In 2015, the MdS organisation announced that instead of a distress flare, weighing almost 1kg, they would give each participant a high-tech security GPS device which would be attached to the shoulder strap of all runners' rucksacks. This allowed organisers and people supporting runners from outside of Morocco to locate each runner every 10 minutes. In case of an emergency, runners could press the SOS button on the device to send an emergency signal - which would be processed within one minute, to identify location. Unless there is an emergency, this device can be ignored completely. Race organisers provide more information on this device on administration day.

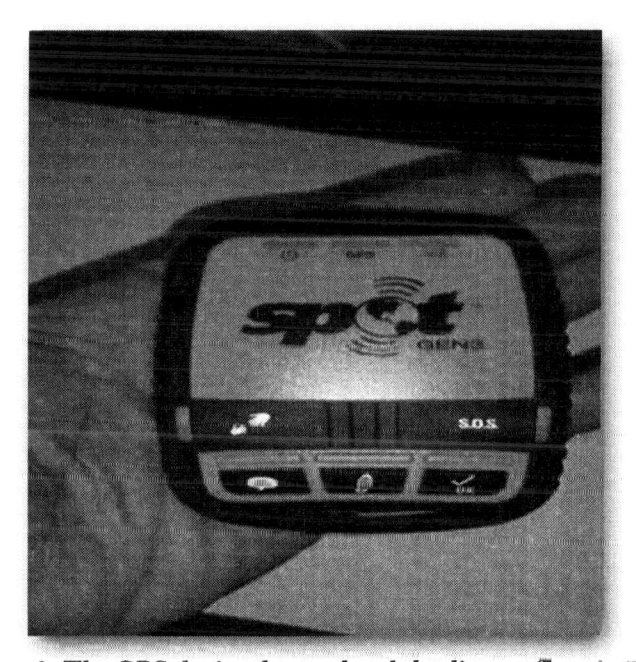

Figure 8: The GPS device that replaced the distress flare in 2015

Rucksack

The aim of a rucksack is not only to fulfil the function of carrying all your items, but also to allow you to carry your supplies in such a way that the weight does not have a detrimental effect on your performance. Research conducted by Genis Pieterse and shared on his blog, www.Push2Extreme, suggests that you should take into consideration the following specifications when selecting your rucksack:

Hip Strap

Since your hips serve as the point around which your balance is centred, they represent a strong anchoring point for any weight you carry. The hip band or strap must sit on your hips, with the aim of resting 80% to 90% of the total pack weight on your hips.

Shoulder Straps

These should be comfortable, broad and well-padded, to prevent the straps from cutting into you.

Rucksack Compartmentalisation

This is essential for balancing the weight of your rucksack around your body. The closer you can pull the heaviest items towards your back, the more your centre of gravity will move slightly back, requiring less leaning forward to remain balanced. This will ensure that you assume the right posture and do not run the risk of damaging your neck, shoulders, back or pelvis from carrying the rucksack.

Back-to-Front Weight Distribution

Another possible consideration for a rucksack is the ability to add a front pouch as a means of distributing the weight and storing items you may need during the day in a way that is accessible. This eliminates the need to take the pack off multiple times during the day, wasting precious time and energy.

Personally, I would recommend going to a specialist ultra-running stockist, such as those identified in the Resources chapter of this book. The people working there often have significant personal experience of ultra-running and can help you make an informed choice, without unnecessary expenditure. As mentioned previously, it is strongly recommended that you train with your selected MdS rucksack to identify any problems as soon as possible. I chose an OMM 25 litre rucksack, which had a detachable mat built into the design. Unlike many of the other ultra-running rucksacks, mine was sturdy enough to withstand almost two years of training and two Marathon des Sables. However, due to my height and build, I had to have the rucksack straps altered to ensure a perfect fit on my small frame. During the 30th edition of MdS, I met a number of runners who suffered very badly as a result of an ill-fitting rucksack. One woman actually suffered open wounds as a result of rucksack straps digging into her shoulders.

You could buy the lightest possible rucksack, designed specifically for the race, but bear in mind that the lighter the rucksack, the less chance it has of surviving your extensive training. It may fall apart, which means you will have to buy another one. No one said that MdS was an inexpensive affair! The only way you can test whether a rucksack is right for you is by testing it consistently throughout your training, with the weight of your equipment.

Sleeping Bag

Your sleeping bag will form part of your overall 'sleep system'. This is essentially the combination of items that will help you get a good night's rest and must be considered to suit your specific needs. The items need to be tested together to ensure that they collectively serve their purpose and contribute to maximum rest.

The temperature in the desert at night can drop to as low as -2°C and conditions can be extremely windy. All race participants will have different requirements dependent on their temperature management. I suffer from Reynaud's phenomenon, which affects the circulation in the fingers and toes quite severely. I could not afford to save weight by switching to a lighter sleeping bag, because I would have been compromising on much-needed heat and comfort during crucial recovery time.

The weight and quality of sleeping bags will vary vastly, but some of the most popular brands used by runners include PHD K series, Lestra Light Ultra 190 and Yeti Passion 3. Your requirements might be quite specific and based on considerations such as height, weight and gender. Again, I would recommend going to a specialist ultra-running stockist to avoid unnecessary purchasing of unsuitable kit. Details of stockists are listed in the Resources chapter of this book.

Head Torch

This is an extremely important piece of your kit. Please do not buy a cheap one! You will need it for finding your way in the camp at night, e.g. for using the toilet and for the night stage of the long day.

I took a Petzl Tikka XP (120 lumen with up to 160 boost/85g), but I also recommend going for a Black Diamond Spot (130 lumens/90g). Both are similar in specifications, run on three AAA batteries and are very reliable, lightweight and easy to use. I advise that you pack your head torch at the top of your rucksack because you will need it immediately upon arriving at the camp on your first night.

Spare Batteries

Do not rely on any old batteries that you have lying around. Your head torch will be an important part of your kit, so you will need the best quality - preferably newly-purchased.

10 Safety Pins

This sounds really obvious, but it's a good idea to hook all of your safety pins together, to prevent dropping or losing one. Try to keep these small mandatory items together, so that the race supervisors can do checks quickly and easily on administration day.

Compass, Accurate to 1°-2°

This is pretty standard, but do you know how to use it? I must confess, the first time I did MdS, I had no clue. I didn't expect to use it and thought it was just a piece of emergency equipment. I cannot stress the importance of knowing how to use a compass for the race. In 2014, even the elite athletes got lost during the first stage, so don't assume that you will always be surrounded by lots of people who know the way or that the route will be clearly marked. In total, MdS only has around 1,300 participants, unlike well-known marathons such as New York or London, which have more than 40,000 runners. The route is not always obvious and may require some navigation, especially if you are at the back of the pack and have a wide expanse of ground to cover. It would be wise to test this knowledge on a few training hikes, so that you can become familiar with its use. I recommend looping a thin ribbon around your compass, so that you can wear it around your neck during the race to make navigation as quick and as hassle-free as possible.

Lighter
You must carry a lighter, even if you are not intending to use cooking fuel. It's a good idea to carry a plastic disposable lighter, since these are lighter than other types.

Whistle
Your rucksack may already have a whistle attached, in which case this will suffice. If you need to purchase one separately, any cheap whistle will be fine. As with the lighter, I advise buying a plastic rather than metal whistle, since these are lighter.

Knife With a Metal Blade
I strongly recommend that instead of taking a penknife, which is likely to have a blunt blade and other parts that you are unlikely to use, you should consider taking a craft knife. When I did MdS for the second time, I found that Robert Dyas sold a pack of three Stanley craft knives for £2.99, which weighed only 20g each, compared to the Victorinox Classic SD Swiss Army Pocket Tool Blue for upwards of £10 and which weighed 100g. You will only need one knife to meet the mandatory requirement, but if you take a craft knife, you can use it in place of scissors, for cutting plasters and for lancing your blisters more effectively. More on that, later!

Topical Disinfectant
The first time I did MdS, I took a mini aerosol can of Savlon spray. However, I quickly found out that aerosols do not work in the desert and therefore recommend avoiding them altogether.

Instead, I suggest taking Friar's Balsam. Friar's Balsam contains benzoin which has two uses for you in the desert; firstly, it can form a mild antiseptic and secondly, it is a very good adhesive. This second point is important, since any adhesives that you take with you are unlikely to stick. This includes any taping on your feet and press and seal bags for your food. Friar's Balsam is incredibly useful for taping purposes because it is almost certain that you will have issues with your feet along the way. I recommend that you decant the solution into a small plastic fine spray pump bottle. You don't need the whole bottle; just half of the contents should suffice for the week.

Anti-Venom Pump
You can buy an anti-venom pump from any pharmacist. It will normally arrive in a plastic box accompanied by a number of spare nozzles. I disposed of the box, keeping one nozzle in a zip lock bag, along with my compass, safety pins and other small mandatory items.

Signalling Mirror

This does not need to be a specific type of mirror. The first time I did MdS, I bought a small compact mirror to take with me. It is worth removing any plastic casing and the additional extra magnifying mirror that often comes in the compact. I saved about 50g of unnecessary weight by doing this, which sounds nominal but really does add up.

Aluminium Survival Sheet

The first time, I took a survival sheet which I had been given at the end of a marathon some previous years ago. The packet was sealed and I didn't think anything of it. However, the second time I did MdS, in a bid to lose as much excess pack weight as possible, I opened up the packet and discovered that the sheet was so huge that I could actually have wrapped myself in it at least twice. As I am only 5"1 and weigh 50kg, this made no sense for me, so I cut the sheet in half, saving myself around 25g. It may not make sense for you to do this, but it is certainly something to consider. Where you can cut weight, you absolutely should; think of it as less weight on your feet and potentially, one less blister.

The survival sheet can also be used as an extra layer at night; there is no reason why the use of this item should only be limited to emergency situations.

Sun Cream

Personally, I despise applying thick, gloopy sun cream to my skin so instead, bought a factor 50 sunscreen spray and decanted 7 days' worth into a plastic fine spray bottle.

200 Euros

This currency serves two purposes: firstly, in the event that you are pulled from the race prematurely, you are likely to need it for accommodation, food, etc. Secondly, after the race you are encouraged to buy as much paraphernalia from the MdS boutique as your funds will allow!

Additional Kit

Toilet Roll, Wipes and Sanitiser

I recommend taking half of a toilet roll, pressing it flat and taking out the cardboard centre and I would also take a couple of packets of Kleenex tissues. I also discovered Wemmi Wipes, which are dehydrated flannels. You simply add some water to hydrate a small towel. These are great, because when they are taken out of their packaging, they are the size and shape of an electrolyte tablet. Personally, I would not take more than one tube of these, minus the tube, to avoid unnecessary extra weight, since these are a luxury. Try to take two hand sanitiser bottles - you will definitely need this at every opportunity and it is also a great way of disinfecting blisters before or after lancing them.

First Aid

According to MdS veteran Genis Pieterse, there are many ailments you may experience while in the desert. For such reasons, your medical kit should be comprised of at least the following:

- two anti-septic hand sanitiser bottles (small)
- fabric plasters (8-10)
- Imodium melts
- Paracetamol
- Ibuprofen
- Friars Balsam
- Zinc Oxide tape

There is no need to take a week's supply of Paracetamol or Ibuprofen, since you can ask the medics en route for more, as required. There are many types of Zinc Oxide tape. I recommend the type that has a good, strong adhesive and that you can tear. Not all Zinc Oxide tape will allow you to do this. There is no need to take more than two rolls.

You don't need to carry excessive amounts of any of the other items on the list; the medical tent in the camp will provide you with anything you need, from tampons to antiseptic wipes and iodine.

I cannot stress enough the importance of looking after your feet carefully and urge you to review the chapter relating to injury prevention and management contained within this book very carefully throughout your training.

Body Glide

Body Glide is very useful if you suffer from chafing and can be purchased from any good running store.

Lip Balm

Many runners forget to take lip balm and end up with horribly dry and cracked lips. The main problem with a standard lip balm is that it is likely to melt in the Sahara heat. I recommend buying lip balm in a stick form that has high beeswax content, such as Burt's Bees. The higher melting point of the beeswax means that the lip balm will be less likely to make a mess of your pocket. Test your lip balm on a heated radiator, if you are in any doubt.

Vaseline

Many first time runners choose to take Vaseline as a lubricant and moisturiser, however there are some crucial flaws with this product. I didn't take this and wouldn't recommend it. Vaseline turns into a greasy liquid in the hot climate, which combined with the silt-like dust that will inevitably start to gather in your trainers, will almost certainly lead to blisters if you use it on your feet. Vaseline will also render any sort of adhesive, such as that on taping and plasters ineffective, which may lead to further blistering.

Cooking Equipment

Like many MdS runners, I chose not to take any cooking paraphernalia at all.

There are a number of reasons for this. Cooking equipment weighs a lot and pre-packaged food is expensive. Research conducted by Genis Pieterse (www.Push2Extreme.com) suggests that satisfaction with freeze-dried food is low, compared with ordinary supermarket food, which you might eat and enjoy on a regular basis. Another thing to consider is the time it takes to cook food. During my first experience of MdS, I found that it seemed to take forever to heat up water and I would rather have had extra time to sleep. Eating pre-packaged supermarket food is far more efficient, and means that you can eat whilst in your sleeping bag, in the morning and at night.

Esbit Cubes (fuel)

You will only need fuel if you choose to cook. Please note that you will not be permitted to take fuel tablets on the plane or pack them in your suitcase, so these will need to be ordered from the official MdS site, details of which will be sent to you well in advance of the race. The Esbit cubes can be collected on administration day, in advance of the race.

Food Items

Guidance on what you should take for MdS is covered in chapter 6 of this book.

Duct Tape

This is great for fixing things and for emergency repairs to torn gaiters. A lot of the terrain that you will be covering will be rocky and this can easily damage your gaiters. I wrapped about an arm's length of duct tape around my anti-venom pump, to avoid taking an entire roll.

Sleep System

Along with food, hydration and injury management, your 'sleep system' will be critical for ensuring that you are in a good state for the next stage of the race. For me, this included a sleeping bag, a sleeping mat, earplugs (a must!) and sleeping pills. I took non-drowsy sleeping pills because I find that I cannot properly function on poor-quality sleep. I took a blow-up sleeping mat (Thermarest NeoAir X-Lite Small) both times I ran the race. Whilst foam mattresses looked better, they were far too bulky for me to carry on my 5"1 frame. I didn't take a blow up pillow, as I had in 2014; because I found that it felt nothing at all like my pillow at home. Instead, I settled on rolling up the running gear I wore during the day. This worked perfectly for me, but I would advise you to test your own methods to ensure that you can definitely get a good night's sleep.

In terms of nightwear, I bought a Tyvek boiler suit and cut off extra length on the arms and legs. However, I disposed of this on day 3 because the build-up of salt and sweat on my body meant that the suit kept sticking to me and was actually very uncomfortable. One of my tent mates suggested sleeping in my running leggings and just changing my top at night, which was perfect in terms of comfort and efficiency.

Walking Poles

I recommend taking walking poles, although there is then the risk of over-reliance on them. You don't want to walk where the terrain will actually allow you to run. It's worth remembering that the less time you spend at each stage, the more time you have to recover at camp for the following day. I decided to use Mountain King Trail Blaze poles, which can be purchased from stores such as Likeys or MyRaceKit. Don't forget to add baskets to the bottom of the poles, which will prevent the poles from sinking too deep into the sand.

Long-Sleeved Top

I found one long-sleeved layer to be adequate at keeping me warm and I didn't need a fleece. When I did feel cold, I used my emergency foil blanket. In terms of a long top, I recommend taking a Helly Hanson base layer, or similar.

GoPro Camera/ Iphone

I took this the first time round, but found it more hassle than it was worth. You can always share pictures with other MdS participants following the race or take your phone, as I did in 2015.

Bottles

Raidlight bottles are sturdy, reliable and used by most MdS runners. Stay well away from OMM bottles because they easily leak and the pouches that come with them are just not up to the job of surviving the Sahara. In fact, the Velcro attached to the pouches is so poor that it didn't even withstand my training.

Slippers

I took slippers to the 2014 Marathon des Sables, but not in 2015. If you take the super light, flimsy slippers supplied by hotels, you're likely to find them too flimsy. I decided that I would rather walk around in my loosely tied trainers than carry the extra weight demanded by sturdier slippers.

Trail or Road shoes

There's a lot of debate around what sort of shoes to wear for MdS. Some runners favour trail shoes for their "gnarly" grip, whilst others favour the road shoe for the extra support. The first time I did MdS, I went for Brooks Ravenna road trainers. I also visited the high street brand, Sweatshop, and had some custom insoles put into them for extra cushioning. I particularly needed these because I was suffering quite badly from plantar fasciitis. My only change was that the second time I did MdS, I bought trainers a whole size bigger than usual, rather than half a size bigger. Brooks Ravenna trainers seem to have a slightly smaller toe box than most trainers and I needed the space to accommodate the bandaging around my toes as a result of accumulating so many blisters. If in any doubt, speak to a professional at a running or ultra-running store, the details of which are contained in the Resources chapter of this book.

Socks

Irrespective of how much you try to protect your feet, you will get blisters. I recommend taking Injinji socks, having tried and tested them during your training first. These are toe socks and the fabric between each toe means that your toes are protected from each other. The extra fabric helps to prevent unnecessary friction, therefore reducing the likelihood of blisters.

Solar Charger

Solar chargers are expensive, heavy and for the most part, more hassle than they are worth. I took a solar charger the first time I attempted MdS, but found it bulky and a bit pointless. I failed to realise that I could only charge an item in the daytime, which was when I was running and needed to use it. For this reason, I settled on an external battery pack.

Music, Garmin 310XT and a USB Power Monkey

These were my luxury items. I took an iPod Shuffle for music. I wanted to take my GPS watch because one of the issues I faced when running MdS the first time was my lack of pacing. I felt that hearing my watch bleep every time I had completed a kilometre would be a good motivational tool. I took the USB Power Monkey (EasyAcc 10000mAh Brilliant Ultra Slim Dual USB (2.1A/1.5A Output)) as my biggest luxury. It weighed 240g, but it guaranteed the charge I needed for my devices for the entire week.

It really is worth testing out your music strategy, because the wrong songs can actually send your stress levels in the wrong direction. I wanted something consistent and upbeat that would match my mood and my regular pace. Personally, I opted to listen to Arabic music since the words were totally unfamiliar, which meant I could listen to the music repeatedly without becoming bored.

The information contained in this chapter is based purely on my own experiences. Anything you choose to take boils down to personal preference and how much you are willing to carry with you for the duration of the race. I limited my kit deliberately to save on weight and because I didn't need a lot of things to get by. My biggest indulgence by far was my gadgets, but I compensated for their extra weight by removing the excess weight relating to every other item as far as I possibly could.

Rucksack Contents

Figure 9 shows the contents of my rucksack for the race. The total weight came to 8kg, which included 1.5 litres of water.

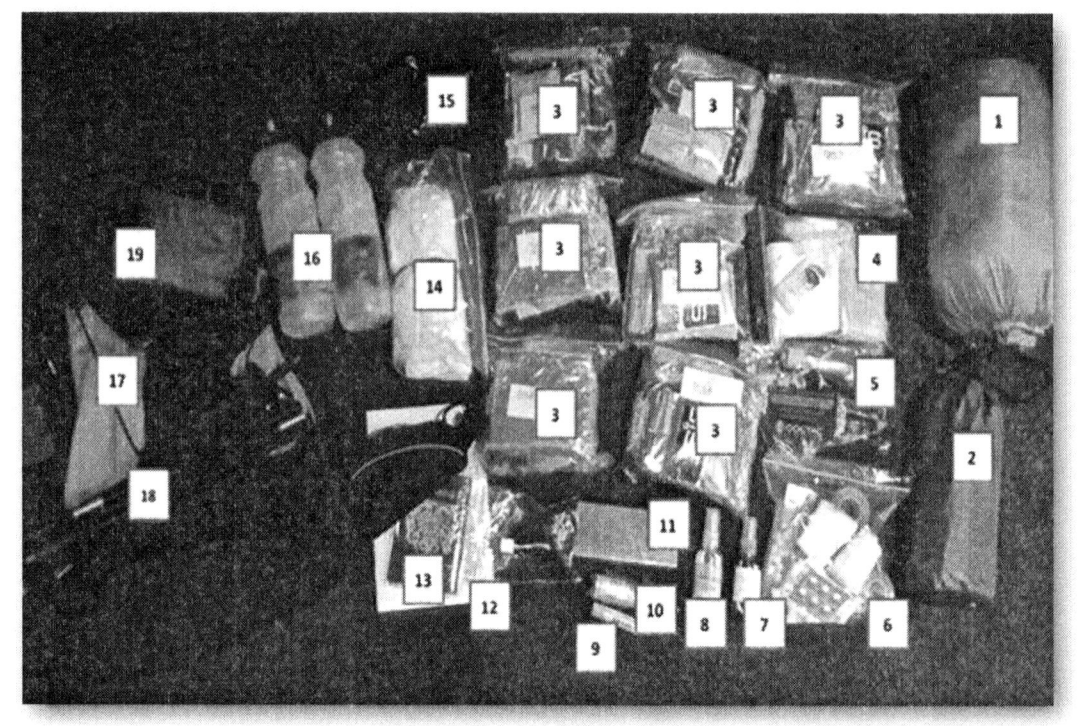

Figure 9: The contents of my MdS rucksack

1. Sleeping bag
2. Sleeping mat
3. 7x labelled food packs (contents explained further in this book)
4. Toiletries pack containing: 15x Wemmi Wipes, 2x travel sized bottles of hand sanitiser, ½ of a full roll of toilet roll, 1x airline tooth brush (snapped in half), 2x airline size tubes of toothpaste
5. Mandatory equipment pack containing: 1x anti-venom pump (in green), duct tape (wrapped around pump), 1x nozzle, 1x credit card sized card documenting insurance details, 1x cosmetic mirror stripped of all casing, 1x small needle with thread and 1x craft knife
6. Medical pack containing: 2x Zinc Oxide rolls, Imodium Melt tablets, Ibuprofen, Paracetamol, sleeping tablets, foam ear plugs and plasters
7. Friars Balsam decanted into a fine spray bottle
8. Factor 50 sunscreen spray decanted into a fine spray bottle
9. Burt's Bees lip balm
10. Nuun electrolyte tablets (second pack is contained in the food packet for day 3)
11. External battery and charge cable for Iphone, GPS watch, Ipod Shuffle
12. Menu list broken down by kcals and weight per day
13. Passport

14. 1x Tyvek boiler suit cut to size (later ditched!)
15. 1x Helly Hanson long-sleeved base layer
16. 2x Raidlight bottles
17. 1x OMM rucksack, adjusted for fit and size
18. Lightweight Mountain Trail Blaze walking poles
19. 1x Welsh flag (in mesh pocket of rucksack)

Review of Example Rucksack Contents

This section looks at how some of the other MdS runners packed their kit and provides a review of what I would recommend doing differently to save as much weight as possible. Please note that these examples were 'in-progress', and therefore some of the compulsory items may not be shown. My review is purely based on how weight could be saved on the items that are shown.

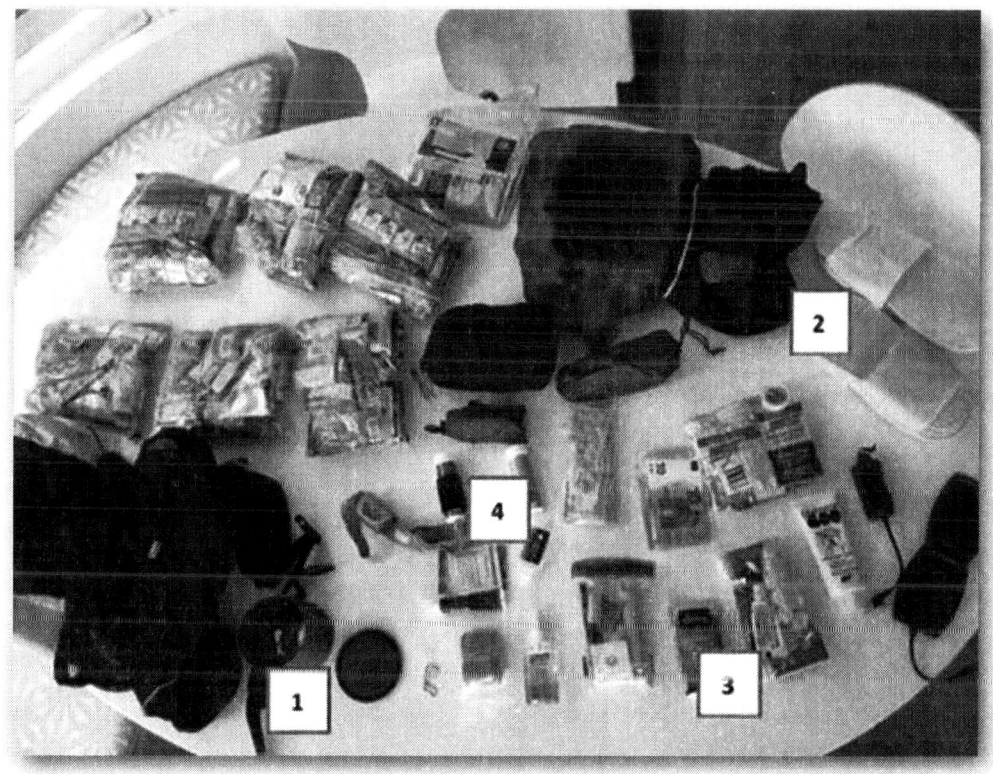

Figure 10: Review of example rucksack 1

Rucksack 1 – Recommended Weight-Saving Changes

1. Avoid cooking to remove the need for a cooking pot.
2. Take one pair of slippers or preferably none.
3. Remove pack of Kleenex and take ½ roll of toilet roll, instead.
4. Decant Nuun tablets from tubes.

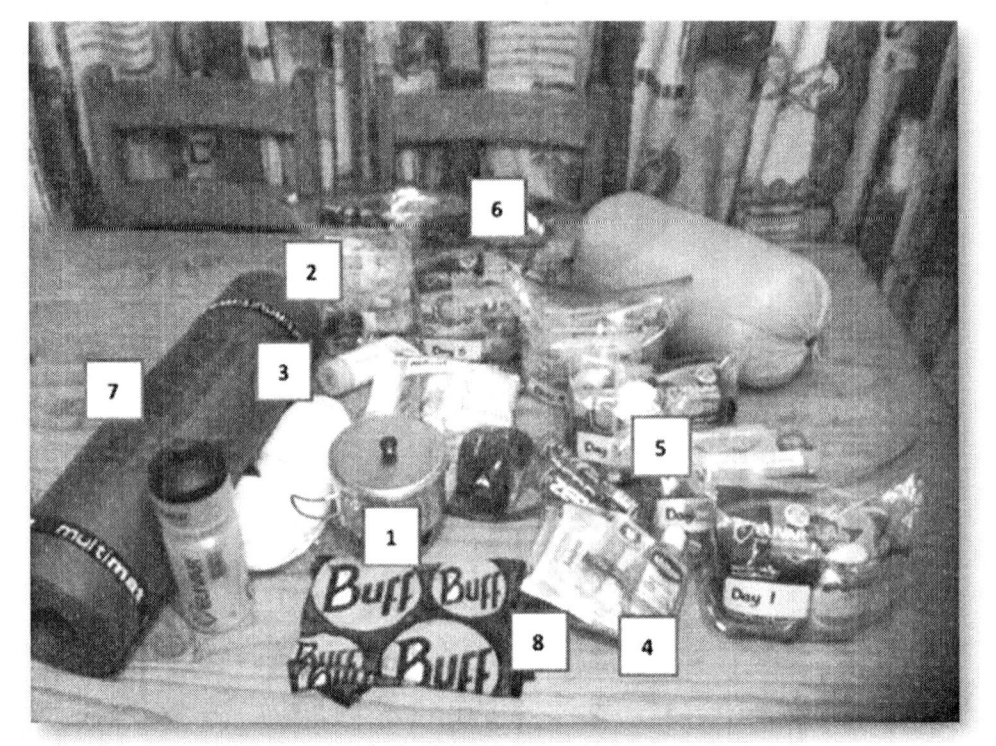

Figure 11: Review of example rucksack 2

Rucksack 2 – Recommended Weight-Saving Changes

1. Remove cooking pot.
2. Remove tub of Vaseline and replace with anti-chafing stick or Burt's Bees lip balm, depending on your reason for taking it.
3. Decant contents of tube to save on weight and bulk.
4. Take a smaller bottle of hand sanitiser.
5. Decant Zero tablets from tubes.
6. Remove packaging from pre-packaged food in zip lock bags– better still, replace these foods with regular, supermarket foods to avoid having to cook.
7. Cut sleeping mat to size, if possible.
8. Swap Andrex wet wipes (in zip lock bag) for Wemmi Wipes.

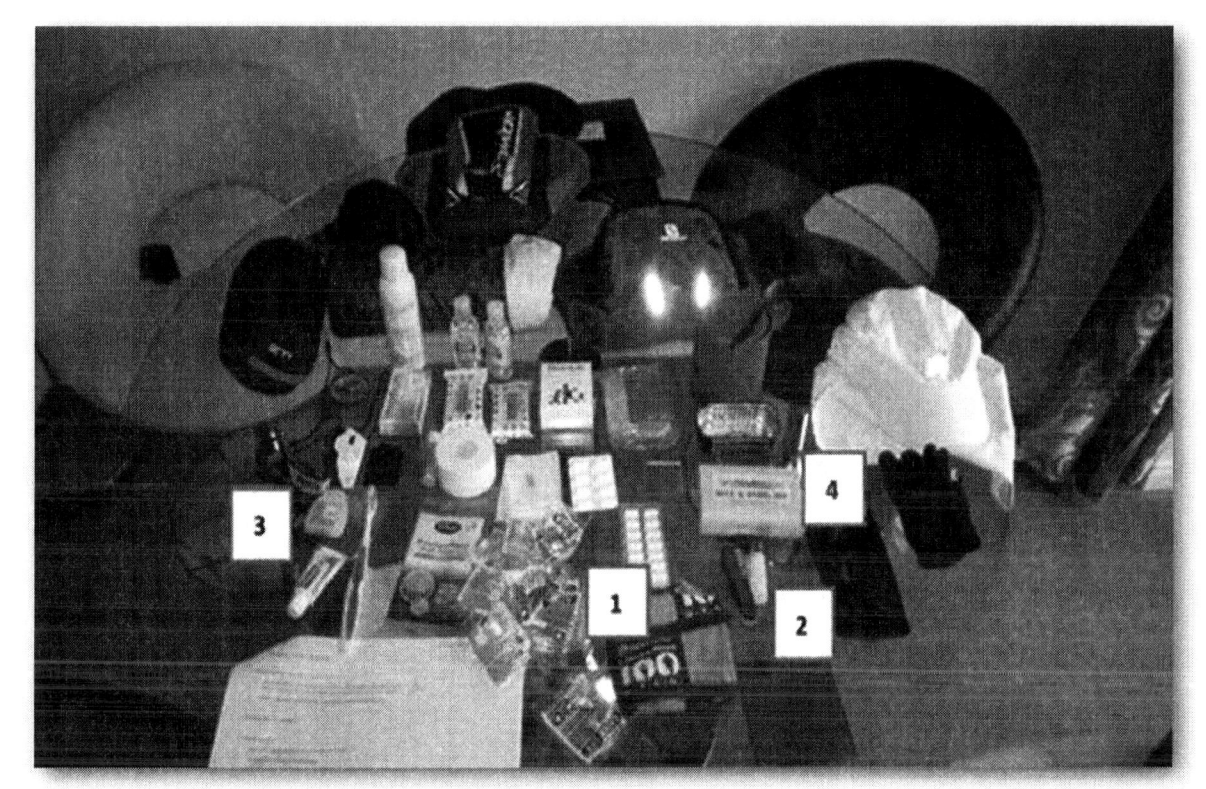

Figure 12: Review of example rucksack 3

Rucksack 3 – Recommended Weight-Saving Changes

1. Remove all pills from blister packs, along with packaging and place in small zip lock bags.
2. Replace Swiss army knife with a simple craft blade.
3. Take tooth floss and wrap it around toothbrush, to save taking the whole container.
4. Remove anti-venom pump from the yellow box and take only one of the nozzles provided.

Hopefully, this chapter has given some clear ideas on how to save weight when it comes to packing your rucksack for the race. I found that when I attempted the MdS in 2014, I really did not need as much kit as I had imagined.

As the realities of the race set in, the things you will care about most will be eating and drinking enough; having appropriate but basic hygiene; feeling warm enough; having fit for purpose feet and sufficient sleep. Everything else is a nice addition.

CHAPTER 6

WHAT TO WEAR

It goes without saying that deciding what to wear in the desert is highly personalised and what works for one person may not work for another.

Here is a sample of what runners from 2015 said, when asked this question, prior to the race:

Runner 1: *"Loose white top and compression shorts."*
Runner 2: *"Calf guards & shorts, short sleeve top and arm sleeves."*
Runner 3: *"Shorts, calf guards, short sleeve top and arm coolers."*
Runner 4: *"Compression shorts and long-sleeve shirt."*
Runner 5: *"Shorts and short-sleeved shirt for run. For the long day, I'll wear a long-sleeved shirt and sleep in compression tights."*

In the meantime, this chapter describes the clothing I chose to wear and the rationale behind my choices.

Headwear

I wore an Inov-8 hat the first time, but found that the curtain that protects the back of the neck did not extend far enough to cover the sides of my face too. I recommend wearing a cap that can be tightened. My Inov-8 cap was too big - even when adjusted, and blew off during the strong wind in the sand dunes on day one.

For the 30th edition, I chose a Raidlight cap, which is perfect in terms of design because it is lightweight and easily adjustable, but most importantly, has a neck curtain which covers the back of the neck, ears and sides of the face.

I strongly recommend taking a buff, which is essentially a tube of stretchy material, available in many different colours and which has multiple uses. It can be used as an eye mask at night, a general rag, a headband and washcloth, too.

Sunglasses

I took Julbo Explorer wraparound sunglasses, which have polarised lenses, making them usable at night. Given that these glasses are wraparound, I found they provided sufficient protection for my eyes during a sandstorm and therefore, found no need for separate sand goggles. You could also use your buff for extra protection, to prevent sand entering your eyes and nose.

Running Shirt
There is a lot of debate concerning the best type of top to wear in the desert heat for a race like the Marathon des Sables. In terms of colour, the best absorbers are also typically the best emitters of radiation, which means that black clothing will radiate better than white. It's worth noting that the Tuareg, who are Berber people with a traditionally nomadic lifestyle, wear mainly black.

Another concern that is often raised is whether it is best to wear a loose or fitted top. There is no conclusive evidence to indicate the best choice. Having tried both, in conditions up to around 30°C, I could not really detect much difference overall. However, when there is a headwind, you will feel the cooling effect immediately with a tight top. Some people wear very loose and some people prefer very tight. I would advise you to try both in a sauna for up to an hour and see how you feel.

I wore a bright purple Inov-8 top for my first MdS and a bright pink Nike Dri-FIT top the second time. These were neither too tight nor too loose, which prevented excessive absorption from the sun. I chose the colours based on my personal preference. In both cases, the tops were long-sleeved, to avoid burning and having to worry about constantly re-application of sunscreen.

Running Tights
I wore Nike Dri-FIT full length tights rather than shorts because I didn't want tan lines and did not want to keep re-applying sunscreen to more areas than necessary. These tights worked perfectly well because I had used them extensively during my training.

Socks
I wore Injinji socks, which I had used throughout my training, with an extra Bridgedale sock over the top. The additional layer was to provide further cushioning and create an extra barrier for my feet from any silt that made its way into my shoes. I also took an extra pair of Injinji socks, which were 2 sizes bigger, to change into during the long stage. The larger sock size worked perfectly because by the middle of the race, I had had to tape up every one of my toes, which increased my requirement for bigger socks.

Shoes
I wore Brooks Ravenna road trainers rather than trail trainers, because I had developed plantar fasciitis, which is a painful condition that is alleviated by additional cushioning.

I chose trainers that were a whole shoe size bigger than my usual size, in anticipation of the need to accommodate plasters for blisters and taping for my plantar fasciitis condition, as well as some degree of swelling. I wasn't concerned about the extra space in the shoes causing problems before these issues arose, because I was intending to wear two pairs of socks and was using custom-fitted insoles.

Whichever type of trainer you choose for MdS, it is important to look for a shoe that has a wide toe box to accommodate any problems you have with your toes. You can test your choice of sock, shoe size and shape by taping all of your toes and seeing how the socks and shoes fit. This should give you a good indication of how you might feel in a worst-case scenario.

Gaiters

Rather than using the MdS gaiters, which seemed to fall apart for quite a few people, I bought Raidlight desert gaiters. If you are intending to wear leggings, I would suggest that the leggings should go over the top of the gaiters, rather than gaiters over the leggings. This means that there is reduced likelihood of sand entering through the tops of your gaiters, which can spell disaster for your feet.

GPS Watch

On both occasions, I took a Garmin 310XT GPS watch. I don't think it matters too much what type of watch you take, but I strongly recommend taking one. It's a huge motivation to hear that little bleep each time you hit a kilometre, particularly if you are running alone.

If you are unsure of what to wear, it is well worth contacting a specialist ultra-running store, such as Likeys or MyRaceKit. Specialist running stores can be helpful to a degree, but I personally found that the sales assistants in standard running stores simply didn't have the knowledge or the experience to assist me with my kit choices for the Marathon des Sables.

My single biggest advice in this area is that whatever you intend to wear, be sure to test it thoroughly before heading out to the Sahara. Two days prior to my flight to Morocco, I discovered that the running tights I was intending to wear for the race, but had not used during training, were far too loose because I had lost so much weight during my training. While a delight in some ways, this would have been a catastrophic discovery while running in the Sahara!

CHAPTER 7

FOOD & HYDRATION

Minimum Calorie Requirements

According to the MdS guidelines in 2015, each entrant must carry 14,000kcal, a minimum of 2,000kcal per day, or risk disqualification from the race.

It's worth noting that 2,000kcal is the absolute minimum and calorific requirements vary based on a runner's gender and size, as well as the energy expended in the Sahara heat. Getting your calories correct is harder than you might imagine. You will need to create a nutrition plan that contains the highest number of calories for the lowest possible weight, so that you get maximum value out of your choices.

Fat Calories vs. Carbohydrate Calories

It is important to recognise that not all calories are equal and that the calories that you consume pre-run, during the run and afterwards should be derived from different sources, so that the calories you consume sustain you in the best possible way. For example, typically you will need slow-release carbohydrates to fuel a workout, quick-release carbohydrates (sugars) during a run and protein to aid muscle recovery after a run.

Moreover, the pace with which you intend to run the race will also play a part in which energy source might work better for you and therefore determine the foods you should take with you to fuel. In 2015, I intended to use a walk/run strategy, which meant that I could easily consume different types of food. Had I intended to run the bulk of the race, my choices would have been limited to gels, powders or Shot Bloks.

When thinking about your running pace, it is also worth considering your pre-run state. Under normal circumstances, it is unlikely that your glycogen reserves will be depleted before a run, unless you follow a low carbohydrate diet, which means that you may be fine eating something like a date once every half an hour. However, if you start running on an empty stomach in the desert, your glycogen reserves are unlikely to be sufficient to keep you going at any speed.

Another important point to note is that what you decide to pack for your race will not only have to sustain your body in terms of your race objectives, but will also play a significant role in your overall psychological state.

In summary, these are my recommendations from personal experience:

- Take 2,000kcal plus any additional requirements based on your gender, size and the energy you anticipate expending.
- The weight of your food items should be proportionate to the calorific value offered. I aimed for at least 4kcal for each gram of food.

- Your calories should come from an appropriate mix of carbohydrates, proteins and fats. Again, the mix is dependent on your gender, size and the energy you anticipate expending.
- You should take food that you have tried before and genuinely enjoy eating.

Food Options

You have two options regarding your MdS food packs. The first is that you buy ready-made ration packs that are made specifically for MdS and similar multi-day races, or secondly, you create your own ration packs. These options are discussed in more detail in the following sections.

Option 1: Buy Ready-Made Ration Packs

Companies such as Extreme Adventure Foods offer ready-made MdS food packs at a cost starting around £100. The food packs contain freeze dried packets of food, gels, bars and other types of fuel which will meet your needs for the entire duration of the race, for a total weight of around 3.5kg. You could also choose to supplement this option with additional items, so that the packs meet your own specific calorie requirements.

This option involves minimal effort, since the consideration around weight and calorific value has pretty much been done for you, thereby saving you time and money. However, this option is expensive and almost always requires you to cook, which will mean the loss of rest time in the desert. It will also require you to take cooking paraphernalia, which as discussed earlier, will mean extra weight for you to carry during the race. Finally, you may not get an opportunity to test the food unless you are willing to spend more money for testing purposes, in advance of the race. In all, I found this to be an ineffective option for me, so I went for Option 2.

Option 2: Make Your Own Ration Packs

I went for this option based on research conducted by Genis Pieterse. Genis' research of MdS participants in 2013 found that food is probably the most personal of all the elements, besides the race objective. Choice of food was also found to be one of the most significant psychological elements that determined the extent to which a runner enjoyed the race. Genis' research showed that only 17% of runners who had taken freeze-dried food were satisfied with their choice, 16% of those runners that had taken a combination of freeze-dried and regular, supermarket food indicated that they were satisfied with their choice, while 100% of those runners that had taken only regular, supermarket and/or homemade, food indicated that they were happy with their choice of food.

These results are indicative of the importance of your personal nutritional choices and how they affect your race experience. Dissatisfaction with re-hydrated food is less about the re-hydration element as it is about how runners assess the effect of their food, pre-race. For most UK runners, being able to assess the effect of the food over a 30km or more distance and in heat exceeding 35°C is practically impossible. The result is that most will not know how the food will taste, what the texture will be like in the mouth or how well it will be digested in these conditions. These variables will have a direct impact on experience and even on performance.

I wanted to test everything and be extremely confident in my choices. I also did not want to waste time and energy cooking, having spent much of the day on my feet.

My Nutritional Plan

Nutrition during Training

There are a number of challenges when it comes to nutrition during your training period prior to the MdS.

During my first attempt of the race, I put very little consideration into how I would fuel my body before, during or after training. This meant that I was not eating enough of the right things at the right time and would then binge eat on the wrong things as my body craved fuel, e.g. refined carbohydrates in the form of junk food, chocolate, snacks, etc. At that time, my rationale was that since I was in training, I could eat whatever I liked because I was burning the weight off.

There are many problems with this approach. Firstly, what you eat during training is not just about maintaining a healthy weight. Eating the 'right' food means eating meals and snacks that will fuel your body, support recovery periods and greatly enhance your training. Secondly, because I had settled into bad habits during my training, I found it difficult to alter them after the race had finished. This meant that when I stopped training, I continued to eat the same way as when I had been running up to five times a week. Unsurprisingly, I piled the weight on, gaining 1.5 stone. Aside from the weight gain, I also found that my energy levels would rollercoaster significantly throughout each day due to my poor diet.

It is outside of the scope of this book to describe nutritional plans in great detail. It certainly is not easy to stick to a formal food plan if you have a busy life, stressful job and lots of training to squeeze in. Overall, I recommend that you maintain a "clean" diet as much as possible. By this, I mean eating natural, unprocessed foods as often as possible and avoiding foods with ingredients your grandmother wouldn't recognise - the names which you can't pronounce. Of course, occasional treats are important for your morale, but you are likely to find that the craving for such food simply diminishes because your new training and diet regime creates such a strong sense of wellbeing.

Most of my training was done before work in the mornings. I found it difficult to fuel very early in the morning, because I often didn't feel like eating and didn't always have the extra hours required to adequately digest a large breakfast. To deal with this, during my training for the 30th edition of the race, I invested in a NutriBullet. I personally dislike porridge, which is almost blasphemous in running circles, but oats were the only thing that would keep me full for long training runs. I used the NutriBullet to create a breakfast shake made of soaked porridge oats, nuts, seeds, honey and protein shake for flavour. Similarly, post-run I would use the NutriBullet to make a protein shake. The advantage of this gadget, which is distinct from a blender and a juicer, is that it will allow you to make nutritious drinks quickly and digest large quantities of fruit and vegetables without removing the nutritional pulp and skin. Maintaining your required nutritional intake is often near impossible when you have an already busy schedule, and I found my NutriBullet went a long way to bridging this difficult gap.

Nutrition for the Race
I felt that my body had enough fat to survive for the duration of the race, so my meals were comprised of mostly carbohydrates and protein to replenish any used stores. I broke my nutrition plan into four categories;

1. Rise – pre-race meal, (mainly carbohydrates)
2. Race – food intended to be eaten while running, (a mix of carbohydrates and/or protein)
3. Recover – post-race recovery shake, (mainly carbohydrates)
4. Replenish – post-race meal, (mainly protein)

As mentioned previously, for my second MdS race, I decided that I definitely didn't want to cook, so freeze dried foods were not an option for me. I had tried this during my first MdS and found myself extremely frustrated having waited for the water to boil only to find that the pot did not allow for a sufficient amount of water as required by the food item and finally, finding that the texture and taste of the food was repulsive in the heat of the Sahara. It was a colossal waste of time, effort and weight in my rucksack and so I decided to completely change my nutritional plan for my second attempt at the race.

I strongly recommend that you do not leave this planning until the last minute. You really must like the food that you are taking with you because after a hard day of running, food should be something that you look forward to. Personally, I don't enjoy gels, Clif bars, Bounce Energy Balls bars, etc., so I needed plenty of time to test alternative items. In the end, I asked my friend, Brie, to make me a breakfast bar to my exact nutritional specifications, containing a mix of nut, seeds and oats.

Do Powders Count?
Every year, runners question whether powders count towards the required calorie count. In 2015, race organiser Steve Dietrich, confirmed that they do. To quote Patrick Bauer's comments on a Facebook feed, *"The rules say 2,000kcal per day. You can bring these as powders or as a brick, as long as it is 2,000kcal and you have the information to support your calorie allowance"*.

Food Breakdown – Calories & Weight
Appendix D, Example Menu Breakdown, shows the breakdown of my food packs for the 2015 race in terms of calories and total weight. I advise you to create a breakdown like this, in case you are selected for random checks and need to provide information about your food choices.

Example Ration Packs
Figure 13 illustrates what my ration packs looked like for each day. You can see that for ease, I packed food by day in zip lock bags. I stuck to these packets, as allocated, until the middle of the race. The reality of the conditions that you are running in mean that you will crave different types of foods and flavours at different points of the race. Although the packets were organised by day, I was entirely flexible about what I would eat on what day. The packs were arranged in this way for practicality and simplicity, only.

Figure 13: Example food packs, by day

Contents of Ration Packs

Figure 14, illustrates the contents of one of my ration packs.

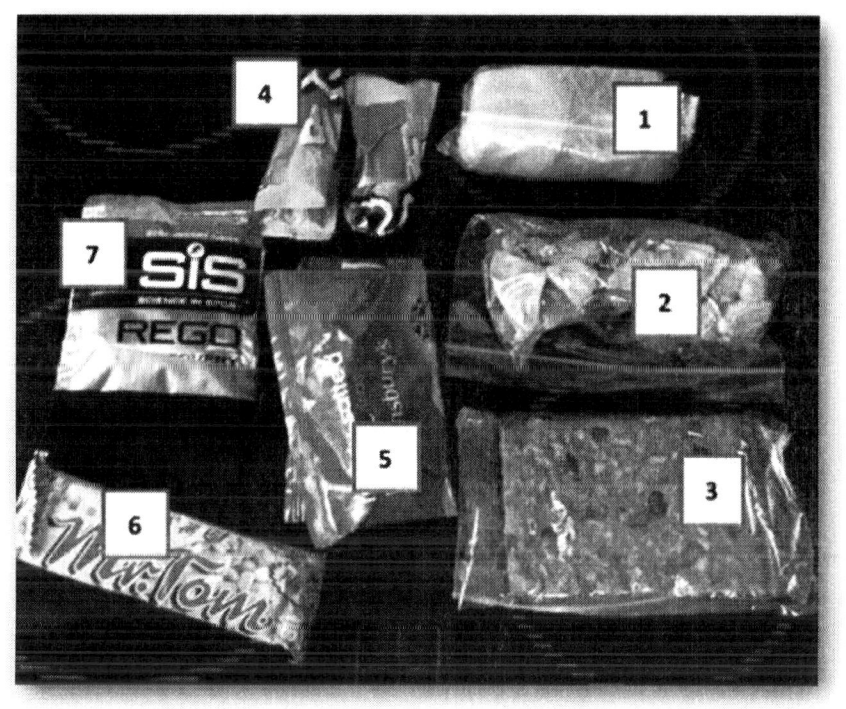

Figure 14: Example contents of one ration pack

1. Homemade "Brie Bar"- this was essentially a flapjack made to my calorific requirements and formed the basis of my breakfast.

2. A selection of dried fruit - I knew from experience that I would be more likely to suffer from constipation than diarrhoea, so I carried dried fruit to eat during the day. This packet contained a mixture of pineapples, raisins and sultanas.
3. My evening meal consisted of x 3 Dr. Karg crackers with Parmesan
4. 2x Pepperamis
5. A packet of salted crisps
6. A bar of Mr. Toms
7. SIS recovery shake for immediate post-race recovery

I must stress that this amount of food would not be enough for most people; I am a 5"1 woman weighing just under 50kg. To re-iterate, your food packs must be based on your own understanding of your requirements based on your gender, size, weight and the energy you anticipate expending.

It's worth noting that when it comes to the weight of an item of food, the manufacturers only list the weight of the contents and not the packaging, which could substantially increase the overall weight you end up carrying.

To avoid excessive weight and bulk, I cut the SIS packet down to size, taping up the opening. I also folded the Pepperamis in half and wrapped them with a small amount of duct tape so that they would be less bulky, and would easily fit into small zip lock bags. For the packet of crisps, I pierced the packet with a pinprick, squeezed out the air and sealed this with some tape so that I could fold it up neatly.

General Ration Pack Recommendations

- Separate food into total packs per day. This means that you will not need to touch the food packs for other days, which will save you time and unnecessary hassle.
- Day 1 breakfast weight is not included in your rucksack weight, so take as much as you like and make your choices different to the other breakfasts you will be taking with you. You will be grateful for variety.
- Proteins and carbohydrates should be consumed at different points in the day.
- Variety is good, and not just in terms of flavours, but textures too.
- Certain flavours and textures don't seem to work very well in the desert. I found that sharp, tart flavours, such as Skittles or dried mango, were really horrible. Gels also taste vile in the Sahara heat. For 2015, I went for natural flavours as much as possible.
- Your body will crave salt more than sugary treats, so you are unlikely to need dessert.
- Take both supermarket and homemade food.
- Packaging should be removed, where possible, to save on weight.
- Re-package using zip lock bags rather than the press and seal bags, since the adhesive on these doesn't seem to work in the desert heat.

Additional Food Ideas

There are a number of nutritionally dense food items that you can take with you. A few examples are:

- Corn wraps with peanut butter and honey
- Ready salted crisps
- Biltong and jerky are great choices for salt and protein
- Dr. Karg crackers are double-baked and topped with parmesan, so perfect because they also retain their shape.
- Dates, raisins, dried pineapple, pears, etc., which are rich in natural sugars are often preferable to artificially-sweetened foods such as gels and Clif Shot Bloks.
- Take condiments, such as Tabasco, wasabi, chilli powder in tiny plastic tubes or bags, if you feel you might appreciate more flavour.

Staying Hydrated

What is Dehydration?

Dehydration occurs when fluid uptake exceeds fluid intake. The human body consists mainly of water. In fact, as much as 75% of your body weight represents the water that is contained within you. Water is used for numerous functions within the body. However, for the multi-stage endurance athlete, water is primarily used for cooling the body through sweating. It goes without saying that extreme exercise adds some level of stress to the human body, as the additional water required for cooling competes with other bodily functions that also require water to perform. The more extreme the event, the higher the body's requirement for water and the more vigilant an athlete must be to ensure that they are adequately hydrated.

Causes of Dehydration

Dehydration is caused by not drinking enough fluids or by losing more fluid than you take in. The severity of dehydration can depend on a number of things, such as climate, level of physical activity and diet. Clearly, for an event like MdS, there is a high risk of dehydration.

Even with a disciplined drinking regime during a multi-stage ultra-endurance event such as the MdS, an athlete is likely to reach a mild state of dehydration from time to time. However, this can be managed very effectively to prevent escalation to something more serious, which could potentially jeopardise your entire race.

Symptoms of Dehydration

Dehydration can be mild, moderate or severe depending on how much of your body weight is lost through fluids. Two early signs of dehydration are thirst and dark-coloured urine. These symptoms are the body's way of trying to increase water intake and decrease water loss.

Other symptoms may include:

- urine becoming progressively darker
- dizziness or light-headedness

- headaches
- tiredness
- dry mouth, lips and eyes
- passing small amounts of urine infrequently (less than three or four times a day)

Dehydration can also lead to a loss of strength and stamina and is the main cause of heat exhaustion. These indicators point to two important actions that an endurance athlete needs to make part of his/her running regime. The first action is to always drink *before* you get thirsty and together with this, to increase your water intake when you do become thirsty at any point. The second action is to urinate regularly. As explained earlier, inability to urinate or the darkening of urine is a strong indicator of dehydration, so recognising this will help you to steer back towards an adequate hydration level.

MdS Support for Preventing Dehydration
Upon arrival at the camp, you will be provided with a set of items, one of which will be a bag of salt tablets. You are instructed to take 3 salt tablets for every 1.5 litres of water you drink. However, the challenge with taking in salt intermittently and then flushing it with lots of water, is that it doesn't remain in your system for very long.

Including electrolytes in your hydration plan ensures that salt is being consumed constantly. To find out exactly how many you will need, you need to understand how much you sweat. In order to do this, take the following steps:

1. Weigh yourself both before and after your run, taking as detailed of a measurement as possible.
2. Take note of exactly how much water you consumed during the run - 100ml of water weighs 100g.
3. To calculate how much you sweat:
    - weight lost (g) + water consumed (g) = sweat lost
    - sweat lost/run duration (hours) = sweat rate

I used a mix of plain water and water containing electrolytes for MdS, because I knew from experience that I would get sick of the taste of them. I carried 2x 750ml Raidlight bottles and put an electrolyte tablet into one bottle and carried plain water in the second bottle. Assuming that you use one tablet for one bottle per check point, you will need approximately 3 tubes of Nuun tablets. You will also have salt tablets provided by the organisers, as back up.

You will definitely get sick of the taste of electrolyte tablets. Your water will be lukewarm and you will be drinking it out of necessity rather than because you feel like drinking. Even so, it is a good idea to test different flavours during your training. Be aware that these tablets will fizz quite vigorously in water and will cause the bottle to leak if dropped in full and sealed. It is best to drop the tablet into the bottle and add a little water first, to allow it to dissolve and to allow the effervescence to settle.

In the event that you really do not like the taste of electrolyte tablets, you could try Elite Electrolyte, which is a flavourless liquid and comes in a handy pocket bottle. However, this has a very slightly oily texture, so will not mix well with water. Instead you could put it directly on your tongue and sip water afterwards.

The Marathon des Sables organisation will provide you with plenty of water during the event. Figure 15 shows my own water card from the 2015 race. You will receive your water card on administration day.

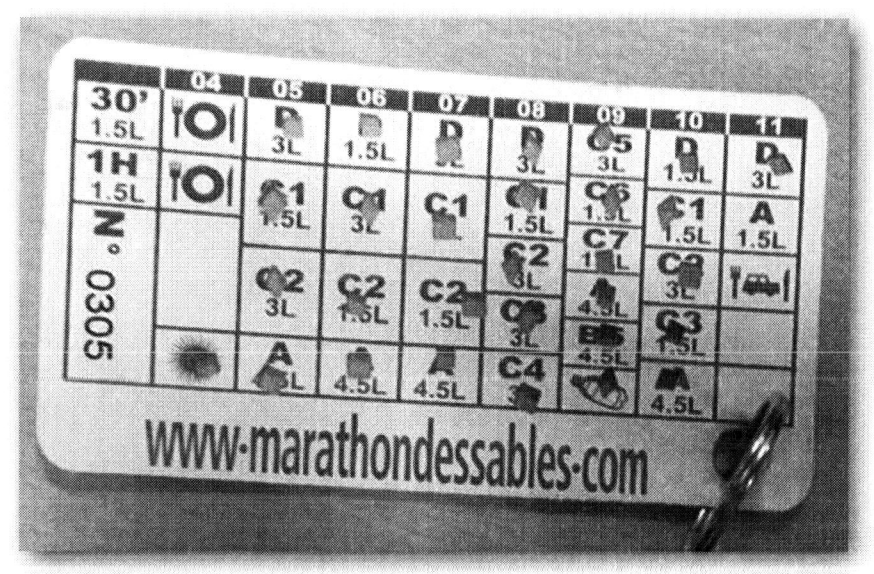

Figure 15: An example water card

In the top row, you can see that each cell is marked by "D", for departure. This shows the water allowance for each morning of the race. These cells have been stamped by race administrators to show that I collected my water rations each morning of the race. Similarly, the following rows, denoted by "C1" and "C2" show the water that was allocated for the check points of each stage and have been stamped to show that I had collected the water. The bottom row, denoted by "A", for arrival, shows the water given at the end of each day of the race. Each cell of this row has also been stamped by administrators.

With a disciplined eating and drinking regime, constant monitoring and adaptation to your environment and by responding to your body's needs, the possibility of becoming severely dehydrated is unlikely. The MdS organisation provides sufficient water to remain hydrated throughout the race, subject to you drinking the water and not wasting it.

The drinking regime in this context refers to a regular small intake as opposed to consuming large volumes, 60 to 90 minutes apart. Given the environment within which these events are undertaken there are always exceptions and variables that cannot be planned for and it is these factors that will require you to manage yourself very carefully, in terms of pace, walk-run ratio, fluid intake etc., to ensure that your dehydration remains manageable. It is inevitable that mild dehydration will happen to every competitor and that from time to time you may even touch on, for a brief moment, something more severe. At this point, you should become more aggressive in your approach to rehydration; drink lots of water, ask for more water, even if a penalty is recorded, and get back in control of your fluid levels.

Of course, you could also experience over-hydration, as I did, two days before the race. As soon as I arrived in Morocco, I experienced a dull and consistent headache. I was drinking lots of water, assuming that the cause of the headache was de-hydration. It was only when a tent mate suggested that I had probably flushed the salts from my system and should probably focus on ingesting more salt, did I finally get rid of my headache.

CHAPTER 8

INJURY PREVENTION & MANAGEMENT

During my training and first attempt at MdS in 2014, I lost a total of eight toenails as a result of poor foot care, and suffered from ITBS as a result of increasing my mileage too quickly, which resulted in other hip-related injuries. I also suffered from plantar fasciitis, which continued for the duration of my training in 2015.

I can tell you from experience that one of the most overlooked aspects of training for MdS is how to prevent injuries and how to manage them when they do happen.

Given the mileage you will be running and the weight that you will have to carry both during your training and for the actual race, it is almost inevitable that you will face various niggles, aches and pains. Ineffective injury management can bring your training to a complete stand-still. Moreover, if a problem manifests itself during the race, it can seriously inhibit your chances of completing the race.

If these issues are diagnosed correctly and managed as soon as they emerge, there's no reason why they should interrupt your training in preparation for the MdS. Obviously, it is impossible to list every single possible injury, but I have included some of the most common injuries you are likely to face as an ultra-runner, along with suggestions on how to best manage them. My advice is based on experience rather than any medical credentials, so in the event that you have an injury that you cannot identify, I strongly urge you to see your doctor or physiotherapist, to avoid unnecessary escalation of the problem. It seems pointless to spend time managing the symptoms of an injury when your time and energy could be better spent fixing the root of the problem.

Common Injuries for Runners

Runner's Knee
Experiencing a tender pain around or behind the patella, or kneecap, is so common among runners, that it was named after them. The repetitive force of pounding on the pavement, downhill running, muscle imbalances and weak hips can put extra stress on the patella. To resolve this, you should try to stick to flat or uphill terrain, and opt for softer running surfaces when or wherever possible. To treat the pain, some experts suggest either taping the knee, using braces or using anti-inflammatory medications, and cutting back on the mileage.

Achilles Tendonitis

This refers to the swelling of the Achilles tendon on your heel and the tissues that connect the heel to the lower leg muscles. It can be caused by a number of things, such as rapid mileage increase, improper footwear, tight calf muscles or even having naturally flat feet. To prevent the pain, it's recommended that you always stretch the calf muscles post-workout and wear supportive shoes. It also helps to avoid hill training if you are experiencing pain, as hills put extra stress on the tendons. Anti-inflammatories, stretching and the Rest, Ice, Compression, and Elevation (R.I.C.E.) strategy are the best ways to aid your recovery.

Plantar Fasciitis

I can talk first-hand about the shocking pain caused by plantar fasciitis. It is the result of the inflammation, irritation or tearing of the thick band of tissue that runs from the front of the heel to the base of your toes, known as plantar fascia. For me, the injury was caused by the excessive pounding on pavements, which led to microscopic tears in the tissue under my feet. If you have had the misfortune to experience it, you will know that this condition is worse in the mornings and results in extreme stiffness of the feet or a stabbing pain in the arch of the foot.

There are a number of things you can do to alleviate this pain. I recommend stretching and rolling a tennis ball or golf ball under your feet and you may also want to consider wearing custom-made insoles inside your trainers. I recommend insoles by FootBalance. I found these insoles to be so good that I wore them throughout my MdS training and have worn them ever since.

One of the worst aspects of plantar fasciitis is that it can totally stall your training for a long, long time. However, this can be overcome by learning how to tape your feet. Having tried numerous other things with no effect, I was extremely sceptical about taping until my physiotherapist showed me how to do it. It is extremely effective. The reason that taping works is that it allows you to take the pressure off the underside of your feet. If your physiotherapist is unable to show you how to do this, there are lots of techniques on how to do this with tearable Zinc Oxide tape on YouTube.

Finally, and this seems like bizarre and unfashionable advice, but I recommend wearing thick-soled slippers, not flip flops, all the time at home. Even if you have to get out of bed to go to the bathroom at night, put on your slippers. Cushioning your feet all of the time will give them the opportunity to heal quickly.

Patellar Tendonitis

This is often referred to as 'jumper's knee', but patellar tendonitis is just as common among distance runners and occurs through overuse, which then leads to tiny tears in the tendon that connects the kneecap to the shinbone. Over-pronation, over-training and too many hill repeats are likely causes. To reduce the risk of patellar tendonitis, strengthen the hamstrings and quadriceps at the gym or at home and ice and rest the knee at the onset of any pain.

ITBS

Iliotibial Band Syndrome (ITBS) causes pain on the outside of the knee, due to the inflammation of the thick tendon that stretches from the pelvic bone to the bone that runs down the thigh to the shin. This is often caused by increasing your training mileage too quickly, downhill running, or by weak hips. I found that foam rolling and strengthening the hip flexors and gluteal muscles through area-specific exercises helped to fix the problem. You can find examples of such exercises quite easily online via Youtube.

Shin Splints

Shin splints occur when the muscles and tendons covering the shinbone become inflamed. Icing the shins for 15-20 minutes and keeping them elevated at night to reduce swelling helped a lot during my training. I also tried to run on softer ground whenever possible, and avoided hills for a few weeks, which put extra force on the shin's tibialis anterior muscle. I also recommend using insoles to support the arches of your feet.

Ankle Sprains

A sprain occurs when the ankle rolls excessively inward or outward, stretching the ligament and causing some serious pain. Curbs, potholes, tree branches or just an unfortunate landing are a few of the culprits that can cause this injury. Recovery may be a little shaky at first, but many experts suggest doing balance exercises, such as single-legged squats, to strengthen the muscles around the ankle. It goes without saying that you should also use the R.I.C.E method, as described previously.

Pulled Muscles

When a muscle is overstretched, fibres and tendons can tear and cause a pulled muscle. Overuse, inflexibility and failing to warm-up and cool down are a few possible causes. These can be prevented through warming up properly with some dynamic stretching and cooling down after a run with a mixture of gentle dynamic movements and static stretching. Again, the R.I.C.E method helps.

Blisters

Whilst I may be stating the obvious, you must wear the correct shoe size and appropriate socks to avoid blisters. In terms of socks, I recommend Injinjis, since they cover each toe separately and prevent friction between toes. The first time I attempted MdS, I suffered very badly from blistering, which resulted in many lost toenails. The lesson is that you must not ignore any sort of foot pain, no matter how small. The implications can be horrific, as shown in Figure 16.

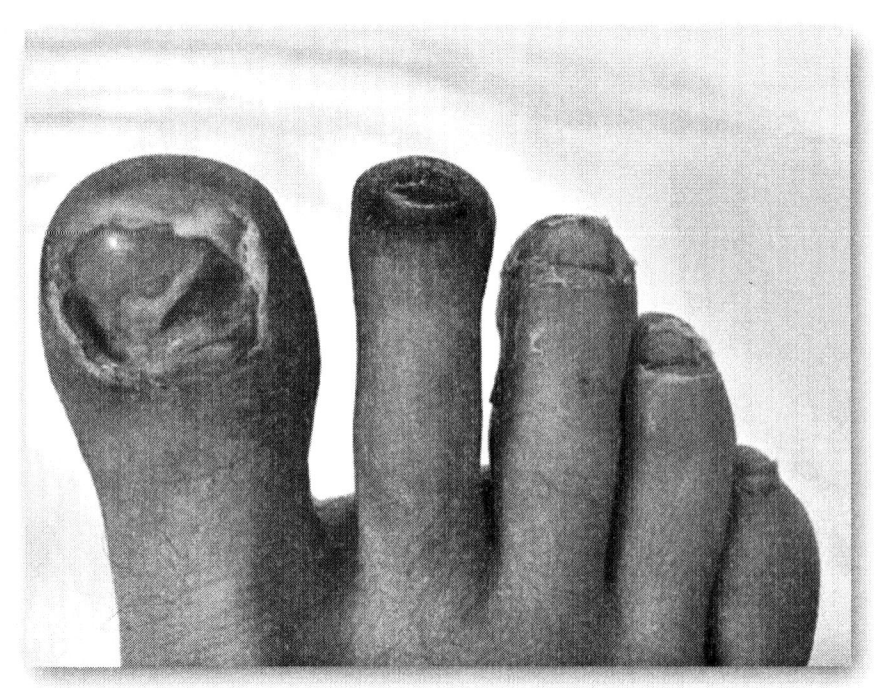

Figure 16: The effects of poor foot management

If you have a fully formed blister, I recommend draining it and covering it with antiseptic and then a plaster. The plaster should be replaced every day.

For MdS, it is absolutely critical that you know how to handle blisters; poor handling during the race can seriously affect your chances of completion. The first time I did the race, I intended to use a pin to drain my blisters. Unfortunately, this just did not work because the hole made by the pin was not big enough to ensure that the fluid was fully drained. The second time I did the race, I took a craft knife, which allowed me to make a very clear, deeper incision, (not too deep, obviously) to ensure that all the fluid could drain properly before disinfecting and covering the wound.

I started to prepare my feet three months prior to MdS with a tanning solution called Tuf-Foot. If your feet are too dry during the race, they may be prone to cracking and bleeding or becoming infected; if your feet are too soft, you are more likely to suffer from blisters. You will need to apply this treatment every day for 12 weeks before the race, and I recommend applying it with a pastry brush rather than a cotton pad, in order to prevent wasting the solution. You can find information on where to buy Tuf-Foot in the Resources chapter of this book.

Lost Toenails

Do NOT pull these off. During MdS, it is very likely that you will lose several toenails from the amount of duress you put your feet under. The toe needs to be taped up and kept clean. You will find that when the toenail falls off of its own accord, there will be a new one growing underneath. If you pull a semi broken toe nail off, you are increasing the likelihood of infecting the area and causing pain that need not occur.

Tips for Injury Prevention

By far, the majority of injuries are self-inflicted and can be caused by increasing running mileage or by increasing pack load far too quickly, rather than incrementally. Often, runners fail to listen to or understand the symptoms of injury, preferring instead to 'run through it', and reasoning that the pain will go away eventually. This is an emotional and irrational reaction - something you must learn to recognise and respond to, in order to stay injury-free. Here are my top tips for injury prevention, based on my own experience, but also on a number of other MdS runners:

- **Increase mileage incrementally** and at a rate of no more than 10% per week.
- **Ensure that your rucksack fits properly** and has a waist belt, so that the bulk of the weight rests on your waist and hips rather than your shoulders. This will help prevent unnecessary strain on your neck.
- **Increase rucksack weight slowly**, so that you are running with approximately 1kg for at least 2 weeks. You can add more weight in increments of 1kg only when your body feels comfortable. If you start adding too much weight too quickly, it will begin to affect your running posture and will possibly push your joints out of alignment, thereby risking potential injury.
- **Keep rucksack weight to a minimum** for the actual race. Some runners carry as much as 15kg on top of their own body weight, which puts enormous and unnecessary strain on joints.
- **Lose weight if you are overweight**. Excessive weight, along with the weight of your MdS rucksack, will place unnecessary strain on your back and joints, making the MdS a very uncomfortable experience and increasing the risk of injury.
- **Balance your load appropriately**. When I first started running with my pack, I was extremely self-conscious of my water bottles, which were supposed to be fixed to the arm straps and on either side of my chest. This location is important though, because not only will it force you to get used to hydrating little and often while running, it will mean that your rucksack weight is more evenly distributed around your body.
- **Lead with your hips**. This means that you initiate the running motion from the centre of your body so that you are driving forward with your knees rather than your feet. This will help you avoid over-striding and to maintain a tall posture.
- **Evaluate your cadence**. Cadence refers to your step rate, or the number of footfalls you take in a minute. This matters because a regular and slightly faster cadence can minimize over-striding and reduce force on the joints.
- **Wear the right shoes**. This sounds so obvious, but you need a shoe that fits your biomechanics. Speciality running store assessments are helpful, but not fool-proof. My advice is to go by comfort. If you have aches and pains after you have run in a pair of shoes, it might be a sign that you are in the wrong shoes. If your shoes feel good, they are likely to be right for you. Aside from this, you will need different types of shoes for different types of running, such as a trainer or road shoe for long runs on pavements, shoes with significant grip for trails and minimal shoes for form drills.
- **Foam roll, stretch, warm up and cool down**. All of these things should be a given for runners, but how many of us actually do them, unless we are injured and have to? A foam roller is a fantastic piece of kit and will pay dividends in helping you to manage and prevent injuries.

The information contained in this chapter does not substitute professional medical advice, but is based on my own experiences and that of other MdS runners during or before the 29th and 30th editions of the race, held in 2014 and 2015 respectively. Please consult a doctor or physiotherapist if you are in any doubt about your injuries.

CHAPTER 9

PRE-RACE PREPARATION

In the months before the race, you will need to think about a number of things, ranging from how to prepare your feet to obtaining a Medical Certificate and ECG. If you are not organised, this can feel incredibly stressful, particularly when you factor in work and family commitments.

To avoid feeling overwhelmed, I created a key milestone plan, which is included in Appendix B of this book. This plan highlights all of the administration, training and other things you need to factor into your MdS preparation.

Creating this sort of plan is one of many ways you can prepare yourself. You are encouraged to use this as a basis for creating your own by adding your own training milestones and by blocking off periods of time when you know you will be on holiday or busy with other commitments. This will give you a realistic idea of how much time you have to commit to training, but also allows you to factor in contingency time for any potential problems that affect your training plan. You will then know exactly what you need to do at specific points in the months leading up to the race.

The rest of this chapter considers specific elements of your pre-race preparation, which have not been considered in previous chapters of this book.

Race Tactics

Although your overall race strategy will determine what your training plan looks like, you will still need some race tactics. Although your race tactics can only really be confirmed once you have reviewed the road book on arrival in Morocco, they are still worth thinking about.

My experiences of MdS in 2014 and 2015 were very different in comparison. For example, in 2014, the long stage was 50 miles, whereas in 2015, the long stage was almost 60 miles. Having failed to complete the 2014 race, I decided that my daily plan for my second attempt of the race would be to:

- Check the length and review the general terrain of each stage or day.
- Check the time limits given to specific checkpoints during the day to ensure that I was several hours within those time limits.
- Run as much as I could when the climate was cooler (i.e. before 12pm).
- Run when the terrain allowed me to and where possible.

For my first attempt of the race, I did not consider any of the aforementioned tactics. At most, I gave the road book a cursory glance and concentrated on meeting people. For this reason, I recommend that you at least put some consideration into your race tactics beforehand and then revisit them once you have received your road book. As long as you are aware of the time limits and where the checkpoints are within each stage, you can vary your strategy to either walk the entire thing, or run it. The decision relating to approach is entirely based on your own comfort levels and preference.

Something else to be mindful of is general safety and precautions during the race. As described in earlier chapters, self-sufficiency is an extremely serious business and you must get used to looking out for any signals or warnings that something is not quite right, whether this relates to unusual headaches, dehydration or any sort of pain.

Preparing Your Feet

Your feet need to be well-prepared for the distance and the terrain you will be covering during the Marathon des Sables. Do NOT go and get a pedicure and ask them to remove all the hard skin on your feet! Your feet need to be tough so that they are less likely to blister, but supple enough to prevent cracking or bleeding. I cannot stress this enough!

There are various ways of 'tanning' your feet – I have heard of people soaking their feet daily in 20 or more teabags. As mentioned previously, I used a treatment called "Tuf-Foot", which is used to toughen the paws of racing dogs. Details of this are included in the Resources chapter of this book.

Medical & ECG

Whilst your medical and ECG is done in early March, I strongly advise that you find out costs associated with these tests from your local GP as soon as possible, in advance of the deadline. The costs for a medical and ECG vary wildly from one part of the UK to another, as may be the case for other countries. If you are cost-sensitive and want to save some money, you should shop around to get the best possible deal. To give you an idea, in central London, you can expect to pay as much as £100 for an ECG and the same for a medical certificate. In other parts of the country, the procedure is free.

It's not unheard of for some doctors to refuse to sign and stamp the forms, because they do not agree with the race based on their own principles. This actually happened to one of the runners in 2015. I suggest researching all of this well in advance of the deadline date for the tests, as stipulated by the MdS organisation. This research will take more time than you anticipate and will definitely add unnecessary stress if done at the last minute.

Navigation

The ability to navigate is important because in sand dunes, where the terrain cannot be marked due to a lack of rocks, trees or shrubbery, you may well need to be able to read a compass.

A Beginner's Guide to Using a Compass
The following section provides brief instructions on how to use a Baseplate Compass.

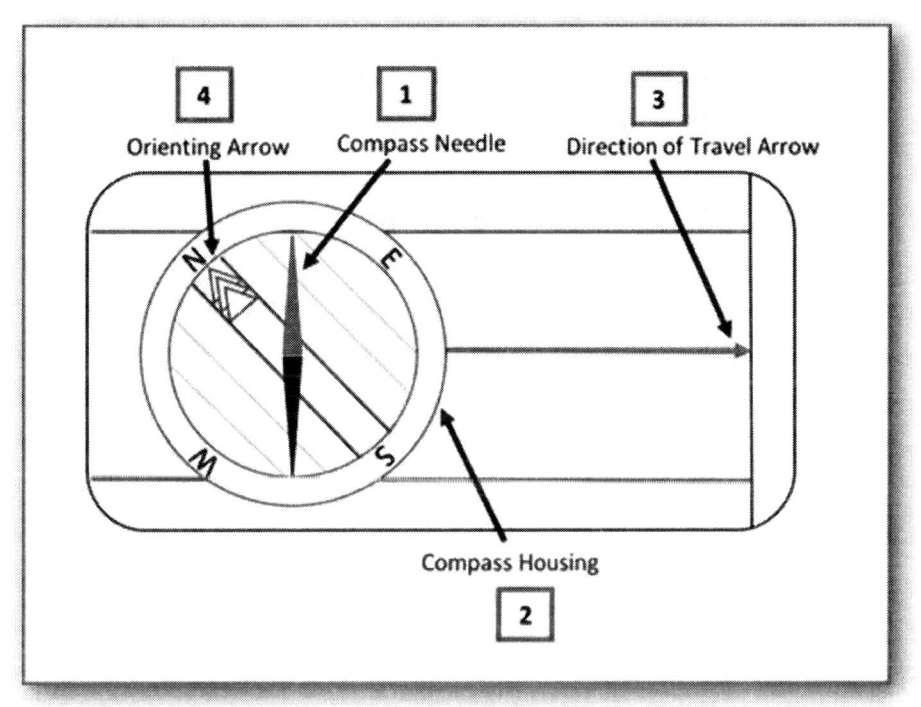

Figure 17: Diagram of a compass

The Parts of a Compass:

1. The compass needle is the red and black, or red and white arrow and always points to the earth's magnetic north.
2. The round moveable dial on the compass is called the compass housing. It usually has a scale from 0 to 360 or from 0 to 400 and allows you to take a bearing.
3. The direction of travel arrow is situated on the base of the compass. This is the line that you will follow.
4. The red arrow on the compass needle must sit within the orienting arrow before you start walking.

Assuming that the MdS road book direction instructs to you to, "Go D/SE (150 degrees) to cross a stony valley", this is how you would follow the direction:

1. Hold the compass so that it is flat and the direction of travel arrow is facing away from you.
2. Rotate the compass housing so that the bearing aligns 150 degrees on the scale, so that it meets the base of the direction of travel arrow.
3. Holding the compass flat in your hand, turn yourself, your hand and the entire compass, making sure that the compass housing does not move. You must do this until the red compass needle sits inside the "N" orienting arrow.
4. When you're certain that you're facing the right way, follow the direction of travel arrow.

N.B. To avoid getting off-course, be sure to check the compass frequently and look out for the landscape features described in the road book - in this case, a stony valley.

Miles to Kilometres Conversion

If you are British, it is very likely that you have been training in miles rather than kilometres. Unfortunately, the road book marks the course distance in kilometres, which means that the Britons often walk around asking, *"What's that in miles?"*

A simple tip is to programme your GPS watch to km during your taper. This means you are in the right mind-set in terms of how you understand the distance.

Heat Acclimatisation

A lot of MdS runners worry about heat acclimatisation in the lead up to the event. One runner I knew went to extreme lengths to create a makeshift heat chamber in his own home, as indicated in Figure 18.

Figure 18: Home-made heat acclimatisation chamber

There are a number of universities across the UK that offer heat chambers for you to test how you fare while exercising, such as Kingston University. However, this is an expensive option.

Personally, I don't think there is much point in worrying about heat acclimatisation until the week before you are due to leave for the Sahara. Anything beforehand is a waste of time and effort. In my opinion, there is also very little value in doing something like Bikram Yoga, since this is a different type of heat to what you can expect in the desert.

I recommend doing a couple of sessions in a sauna in the last few days of your training, if you feel you must do something. I did this for 30-40 minutes at a time and I had no problem with the heat during the race in 2014 or 2015.

Filming and Photography

To find out about photographers, you should contact MdS directly. A lot of participants in the MdS Facebook group tend to set up Dropbox folders to share their photos after the event, so there is not necessarily a need for you to employ a professional photographer.

Friends and Family

To find out about the latest deal for having friends and family come out to support you, you should email the MdS organisers directly via their website, as this package may be subject to change.

Tracking Your Progress From Home

The MdS website provides family and friends with several means of tracking a competitor's progress during the event and keeping them up-to-date with general daily news and photos.

Here are the instructions on how to use the tracking function on the website, courtesy of my friend Paul, who tracked me during the race in 2015:

"You need to be on the correct website; for the 2015 race, this was www.marathondessables.com. The default language is French, but if you click on the Union Jack flag in the right hand corner of the screen, the language will switch to English.

To track competitor progress during a stage, go to the home page and select the "Track Time" page from the menu. Enter the competitor number and the search results will show the competitor name and number and a list of the times for each check point that has been reached. Apart from the Charity Stage on the final day, all stages have multiple check points, so progress can be seen by how many check points have been reached."

For the 2015 race, a new GPS tracking system was trialled. Each competitor was given a small GPS tracker to attach to his or her rucksack strap, which transmitted a location signal every 10 minutes. This location data was used to show a runner's position between checkpoints. The 'Live Tracking' page allowed friends and family to search runners by their race number. However, instead of a table of check point times, the tracking data is used to display a flag on a Google Earth-style map, at the most recent location, along the route the runner has taken, which is represented by a bold line cutting across the desert.

The flag on the map is often a little delayed compared to the checkpoint times, so it is worth making friends and family aware of the possible time delay if they are planning to use the live tracking as a guide for when to start watching the live webcam of you at the finish line.

Another really good feature of the website, for friends and family who want to immerse themselves more into MdS, is the collection of daily photos and videos. The videos in particular are far more effective than words at conveying just how hot, dusty, windy, rocky and steep the terrain can be. I have it on good authority from my friend Paul, that the helicopter shots of an ant-like line of competitors climbing up a huge jebel and the collection of relieved runners who have reached the top, pausing for a rest, or to revel in their achievement, are amazing.

CHAPTER 10

RACE COUNTDOWN & COMPLETION

Those long, arduous months of training are finally over and it's time to leave for Morocco. In 2014, just prior to my first attempt at the race, I experienced a mix of panic, fear and excitement. I questioned whether I had trained hard enough and whether the training had been appropriate, given what I was about to face. I packed and re-packed my rucksack many, many times and yet still wondered whether I was carrying too much.

I did not experience the same sort of anxiety prior to my second attempt at the race, in 2015. I attribute this to having a much clearer idea of what I was doing, and a better-informed training and race strategy overall.

Although you will experience more self-doubt than you have probably ever known, you must put your best foot forward, keep calm and literally, carry on. This chapter is designed to help alleviate some of the anxiety associated with the details of the race by revealing what you can expect once you leave the U.K. or country of origin.

Race Logistics

The Marathon des Sables is a massive logistical affair, more so than you can possibly imagine. Just to give you a sense of scale and the level of organisation that is involved, here are some interesting facts about the race.

MdS Facts

Whilst the New York marathon hosts around 45,000 runners and the London marathon hosts around 37,000 runners each year, the MdS only has around 1,300 runners on average each year. However, the support required for relatively few competitors is huge and includes:

- 23 buses
- 2 helicopters
- 1 Cessna plane
- 4 quad bikes
- 1 incinerator lorry
- 80 Saharan tents
- 200 Berber tents ("bivouacs")
- 15 tonnes of logistical equipment
- 2.5 tonnes of medical equipment and supplies
- 400 technical and logistical staff
- 60 press, radio and TV journalists

- 52 doc trotters (foot doctors)
- 50 people to put up the tents
- 28 race controllers
- 100 TV channels broadcasting in 200 countries
- 120,000 salt tablets
- 120,000 litres of mineral water
- 150 litres of disinfectant
- 2,500 antibiotics
- 6.5km of Elastoplast
- 2700 band aids

As you can see, the scale of operations is pretty spectacular. You will inevitably feel immensely proud of being a part of this unique event when you arrive on camp.

Camp Layout

Figure 19 gives you an idea of what the layout of the camp will look like. You will have a race number, which you will wear on your chest and on your rucksack, but you will also have a tent number.

The key immediately below Figure 19 indicates the likely location of runners by nationality. This diagram should give you a very good idea of what your 'home' will look like for the duration of the race.

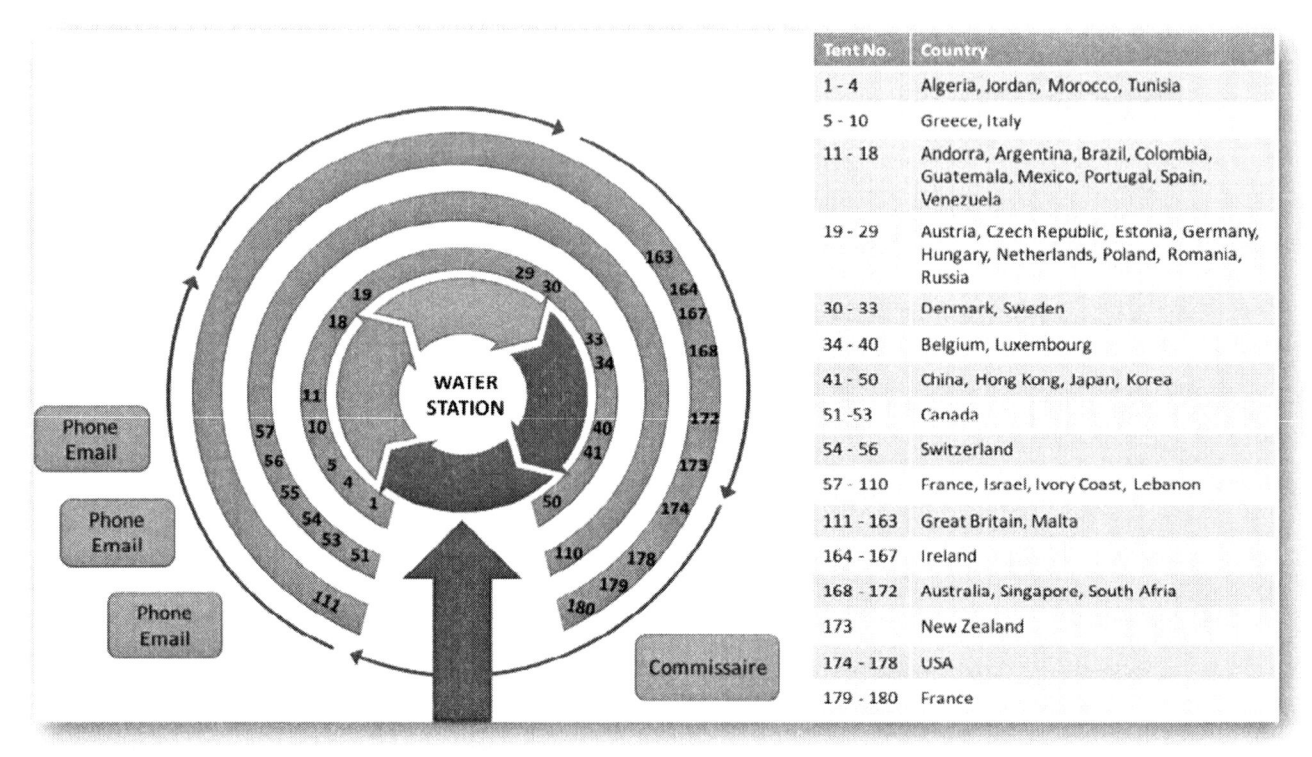

Tent No.	Country
1 - 4	Algeria, Jordan, Morocco, Tunisia
5 - 10	Greece, Italy
11 - 18	Andorra, Argentina, Brazil, Colombia, Guatemala, Mexico, Portugal, Spain, Venezuela
19 - 29	Austria, Czech Republic, Estonia, Germany, Hungary, Netherlands, Poland, Romania, Russia
30 - 33	Denmark, Sweden
34 - 40	Belgium, Luxembourg
41 - 50	China, Hong Kong, Japan, Korea
51 - 53	Canada
54 - 56	Switzerland
57 - 110	France, Israel, Ivory Coast, Lebanon
111 - 163	Great Britain, Malta
164 - 167	Ireland
168 - 172	Australia, Singapore, South Afria
173	New Zealand
174 - 178	USA
179 - 180	France

Figure 19: Layout of camp and location by nationality

Figure 19 shows that the outer ring of the camp, from tent 111 to tent 163 is occupied by British runners. The elite athletes, most of whom are typically Moroccan runners, tend to be located in the inner circle of the camp.

The following section of this chapter considers the overall itinerary and the stages of the actual race.

At the Airport

The race itinerary may vary from one year to the next, so the itinerary-related information in this chapter is based on my experience of running the MdS on two occasions in two consecutive years. As a confirmed entrant of the race, you will receive itinerary information a week or so before heading to Morocco. The following information should be considered as indicative only:

A special flight is chartered from London Gatwick for the British entrants heading out to the Sahara to run the MdS. Your end destination may be Errachidia, (pronounced Ri-Shid-Ee-Yaa), as it was in 2015, but it may also be Ouarzazate, (pronounced War-Zaa-Zat), as in 2014. If you are a UK entrant and live outside of London, you may want to stay in one of the hotels near Gatwick airport the night before, and use the free shuttle service to the airport. This will also give you the chance to meet up with other runners before arriving in Morocco.

Once you arrive at the terminal check-in, you will be greeted by MdS race representatives.

Useful Tips

- **Carry key items as hand luggage.** It is strongly advised that you pack your running shoes and your race rucksack with essential contents as hand luggage on the aircraft, but without exceeding your hand luggage allowance. In the unlikely event that your baggage goes astray, a whole kit can usually be put together with the generosity and help of other competitors, but shoes are not something that can be easily replaced. In 2015, one British competitor failed to follow this advice and had to rely on donations from other runners.
- **Carry one suitcase and one rucksack.** On the day that you fly to Morocco, you can wear ordinary clothing. The next day, on camp, when the medical and equipment inspection day takes place, your suitcase with your travelling clothes and personal belongings will be collected and sent by truck to the hotel where you will be staying. Your luggage will be stored in a locked room until you arrive on Saturday, following the race. I would suggest that you take a suitcase that can be easily identified from storage.
- **Carry your passport and credit card with you throughout the race**. Do not put them in your suitcase for storage during the race. It is also worth bringing a photocopy of your passport. This will make departure from Morocco easier in the event that you lose your passport.

In Morocco

Once you arrive in Morocco, expect a long wait to get through customs. From the airport, you will be loaded onto a coach and once inside the coach, you will be handed approximately 3 litres of water, toilet or sanitation bags, the MdS road book and a packed lunch. You can expect to wait on the coach for at least 2-3 hours while the other coaches are loaded with competitors.

Your road book is the bible that describes the terrain; it directs you through the race and is therefore fundamental to the event. You *must* look after this carefully.

Before the coach leaves, many people walk around outside. If you have not yet decided on tent mates, now is a good time for you to talk to people and decide on your tent mates.

The coach trip from the airport into the Sahara will take around 5-6 hours and you will arrive in darkness, which is why your head torch, with pre-inserted batteries, should be kept at the top of your rucksack.

Useful Tips

- **Highlight directions in your road book.** When you open your road book, you will see that all of the directions are in French first, then in English. When you are running and are extremely tired, your eyes will literally be fighting to read these directions. As mentioned previously, it's worth highlighting the directions that appear in English, assuming that English is your first language, of course!
- **Adjust your watch.** Change your watch so that it reads in kilometres rather than miles, although ideally, you should do this during your taper period.
- **Check how to use your compass.** This is a great opportunity for you to ensure that you know how to use it. If in doubt, ask around other competitors.

At the Camp

You will spend the first night in pre-erected tents. A packed meal will be provided. Unfortunately, the organisers do not cater specifically for vegetarians or those with special dietary requirements, so you may wish to supplement this meal with your own food.

When you arrive at the bivouac on Friday, it will be getting dark, so finding tents is easier if you already have a group of 8 people. The UK tents are on the outer circle (111-163 & Ireland 164-167), and race administrators will greet you and help direct you to the tents allocated for your nationality.

Administration Day

During the first day at camp, you will need to fill in a form that confirms that you have all of the mandatory equipment, ECG and medical forms required. You will also need to confirm the number of calories you have with you for the duration of the race. On completion of this, you will go to the administration tent with your suitcase, which will be taken back to the hotel that you will be staying in following the race.

Once your administration form has been checked, you will be given a race number and told how to attach it to your t-shirt and your rucksack, such that it complies with race regulations. Your bag will be weighed, and the medics will check your ECG and medical certificate and provide you with 120 salt tablets for the race. The medics will also advise you on how to take the tablets in terms of amount, frequency, etc.

and provide you with a water card for use at checkpoints. Every time you reach a checkpoint, you collect your water and the race administrators will clip your tally card to prove that you have collected your allocation. This will be done every time you collect your water rations at checkpoints. However, the responsibility to ensure that the card has been clipped lies with you. You will also be given a supply of water at the beginning of every day, during each checkpoint and at the end of each day. The amounts vary from 3 litres to 4.5 litres at the end of the day.

The organisers mark the cap of every one of the bottles allocated to you with your race number. This is so that all litter can be traced back to individual runners and time penalties can be applied.

The medics will also provide you with a medical card, similar to the water card. In the event that you need medication, a medic will mark the card, allowing them to keep track of the dosage of any medicines you have been given and the frequency with which you are taking them. Obviously, if you take your own medicines, this will not be tracked because the responsibility of dosage taken lies with you rather than the organisation.

You will be given a transponder, which you must fasten with Velcro around your ankle and secure with a safety pin. This device allows you to be tracked between checkpoints. The moment you cross the line at a checkpoint, it will make a 'bleep' sound to register your arrival. A Gen 3 GPS device will also be attached to the strap of your rucksack. As the device is secured, the administrator will explain that the only reason you will need to touch it is to press the SOS button in the event of an emergency.

Once you have handed over your suitcase and successfully gone through the mandatory administrative tasks, you are likely to feel very relieved; from this point, you will only have to look after yourself and the kit that you are carrying in your rucksack.

Useful Tips

- **Keep tight management of all of your kit**. This sounds obvious, but when everyone is spreading out their belongings every morning and repacking their bags, it is easy for something to go astray. In the past, runners have risked disqualification by losing key items of their kit, such as a head torch.
- **Toilet arrangements.** Outside the outer ring of the bivouac there are stalls, which represent toilets. You will be given large brown biodegradable bags, which you will use for toilet purposes. In these stalls, you will find a toilet seat to which you can clip your toilet bag. A rock must be thrown into the bag prior to use, to ensure that when you stand up, the air does not lift out the contents of the bag. When finished, you need to remove the bag, tie it and dispose of it in the large metal bin, which is kept outside the toilet stall. It sounds unpleasant, but this is as hygienic as it can be, given the conditions.
- **Overall hygiene.** You *must* get into the habit of using your hand sanitiser to clean your hands after using the toilet and before preparing any food. If you drop any food on the tent rug, bin it. The rugs are a haven for bacteria and considering bacterial infections from poor hygiene and bad foot care are a major cause of race failure, you do not want to skimp on the hand sanitiser.

The Race

If you have managed to sleep, you will probably wake up excited and more than a little nervous at the start of your MdS adventure - and the culmination of maybe a year of intensive training and preparation.

Be warned that the Berbers will start to pull the tents down early, because they need to dismantle the entire camp to take it to the next location for the end of the first stage. While you are still relatively fresh, I recommend getting your morning routine sorted; this includes dressing, washing, eating breakfast; packing your kit and applying sunscreen. You must be quick and efficient about completing your morning routine, because this will go a long way in minimising stress for you immediately before the race.

The camp will gradually awaken between 6am and 6.30am and the time before you head to the start line will pass incredibly quickly. If you have not invested enough time in checking and taping your feet, going to the toilet and completing the other necessary morning rituals, you risk suffering needlessly during the race.

You will need to collect your morning water rations (3 litres) between 6.30am and 7.30am. In order to do this, you will need your water card so that it can be stamped on receipt of the water. Other things you will also need to do include: distributing your race food across easily-accessible pockets in your bag; filling your water bottles, including one with electrolytes; and finally, reviewing your race handbook.

One problem is that sorting and taping feet as you progress through the race can take as long as 40 minutes, which impacts everything else in your routine. Additionally, everything takes a lot longer than you could possibly imagine, because you are tired, your feet hurt and your mind is in over-drive due to the adrenaline surging through your system.

Expect to be kept waiting for some time at the start of the race, while Patrick Bauer gives a long speech in French which nobody can hear due to the helicopter hovering overhead. Also, expect to sing "Happy Birthday" to those mad people spending their special day doing the race.

The first day is generally shorter and easier, so use it as a 'warm up', to acclimatise to your surroundings and get used to drinking and eating snacks regularly.

Your road book will give you clear directions on which way to head and the course will be clearly marked with pink chalk or spray on rocks or bushes.

You can usually get a feel for how tough the next stage is going to be by how much water is given at each checkpoint. One trick I learnt quite early on is to tip any leftover water into my hat and into the back of my shirt for some relief from the heat. All check points have tented areas for competitors to rest for a while out of the fierce sun, to tend to feet or to sleep in during the long stage.

At the end of each day, emails that have been sent to competitors during the day are printed off and brought round in the evening. Evenings can be great fun, but most nights, you will be ready to sleep by 8pm to ensure that you are sufficiently rested for the next stage.

The next two stages will be similar in terms of length and difficulty, although you can expect the sand dunes to make an appearance. Also expect rocky mountains or jebels, which have rough, rocky trails, ascents and descents.

There will also be plenty of huge, flat, featureless stony plains to walk across - the type that you see in the distance, but which you still have not been able to reach four hours later. Your compass navigation skills are essential here, because even a slight deviation from route can disrupt your course. Vehicles with support staff drive past every so often, checking on competitors. It's worth giving them the thumbs up to indicate that you're okay.

There will be dark periods in this race. If you have music with you, download tracks that make you feel good and use them to get through the rough times. Many runners took a letter of encouragement from a loved one or a special photo to pull them through. Little touches like this can make a real difference and can even stop you from throwing in the towel when the going gets very tough.

The Long Stage
This is usually 50-52 miles. You have approximately 34 hours to complete this stage. However, the quicker you complete it, the longer you have to rest before the marathon stage.

There is a cut off time to reach checkpoint 4, so I concentrated on getting there without stopping for too long at check points 1-3. My intention was to rest at checkpoint 4 if needed. Some people, like myself, slept at check point 4 for the night and finished in daylight the next day, whilst others had a brief stop and then pushed on through the darkness.

When it starts to get dark, you will be given a glow stick to attach to the back of your rucksack. Glow sticks will also be used to mark the route, although you will still need your head torch.

Finishing the Race
Once the long stage is over, the next challenge is the marathon stage. When you've completed the long stage, you have broken the back of the race. However, there will still be 26 tough miles on top of what will already have been covered in the previous few days.

Once the marathon stage is finished, there is definitely an air of celebration around the camp. You would be unlucky not to finish now as the last day is seen as a mere 'fun run' for charity. You will also get to experience a bit of culture, as a complete classical orchestra is shipped out to the desert and a stage is constructed for a concert.

Savour the last day. You might want to just get to the end, but you are reaching the climax of a unique and unforgettable experience. I wanted to treasure these memories for a lifetime, having formed a bond with a diverse group of people.

All too soon, the finish line will be ahead of you and your well-earned medal will be hanging around your neck.

Your End-of-Race Picture

This is quite a strange thing to consider, but what does your iconic MdS completion picture look like? Do you want to be pictured holding a flag? Or perhaps smoking a cigar? It's worth thinking about this one picture that will encapsulate everything you have been working towards for the best part of eight months - or possibly more. I found that this also helped me visualise completing the race, as well as helped to carry me through the toughest parts of my training plan.

Figure 20: Immediately after crossing the finish line

You may want to consider how you want to store or present your medal following the race. This may seem like over-planning, but I found that thinking about these things actually helped me to visualise making it all the way to the end.

Figure 21 shows how I decided to present my medal. After such hard work, there was no way that I wanted this medal to be tucked away in a cupboard somewhere!

Figure 21: My MdS medal and special memories

I decided to put my memorabilia into a shadow box, which is essentially a picture frame that has depth. The sand and some of the rocks in this box are from the Sahara. The box also showcases some other rocks I collected from the previous adventures that lead me to the MdS, such as Mont Blanc, Everest Base Camp and Kilimanjaro.

After the Race

At the end of the MdS, you will be taken to your hotel by coach, which may be a 6-hour drive away. Once you get to the hotel, you will be stiff, sweaty and very tired, but you will still need to queue up to get your room key and collect your bags. You will need a lot of patience at this point, as there will be many competitors trying to check in at the same time, all desperate for a shower before dinner.

The next day is a free day, but you will need to go and collect your finisher's t-shirt from a nearby hotel. You will also have the chance to buy any MdS memorabilia to take home.

Expect another early start on the final day as you leave for the airport, and also expect to feel every emotion under the sun - from elation at having completed the race, to sadness that your adventure has come to a close.

Life After MdS

More likely than not, you will feel a little lost, having completed the Marathon des Sables.

After my first experience of the race, I felt mentally and physically traumatised for quite some months. It was surreal to experience the Sahara Desert and then, days later, walk into an office environment. I felt almost as though I had simply imagined being lost in the desert!

Following my second attempt, and having successfully completed the race, I felt an immense sense of pride at finally having the MdS medal hanging around my neck.

One of the things that will strike you after the race is how depressed your fellow runners look - far from euphoria, there is almost a sense of, *"What do I do now?"*, *"How will I fill my time?"*, and more importantly, *"What's bigger than this?"*

In my experience, the people who run the MdS tend to plan something almost immediately after the race. I knew more than ten people who were intending to run the London marathon just a week or so after completing MdS. Others planned to run other extreme ultra-marathons or complete an Iron Man race or three. The list of possibilities is endless.

Personally, after two years of training for the MdS, my plan was to take a holiday and then complete my book, so that I could share my experiences with you.

Completing the MdS has meant closure for me. In some ways, it also represents the beginning of greater things. After all, our potential as human beings is infinite, and far greater than any race.

EPILOGUE

Simon and I had planned to return to Morocco to run the Marathon des Sables for a second time in 2015. However, in January, a few months before the big event, Simon told me that he had developed a severe hip injury. Simon's injury became progressively worse - so much so, that he was unable to walk without limping. During the course of several months and over a series of phone calls, Simon and I gradually concluded that he should not run the race and potentially risk severe injury or permanent damage. By the end of March, it was confirmed that Simon would not be joining me. Unfortunately, this meant that he also lost all race-related fees.

Some weeks later, Simon sent me a text message, saying, *"You're not going to believe this. I went to Cheltenham dog races and won £3,000!!"* This almost covered the cost of his MdS race entry and since Simon's flight had already been booked as part of his race entry, he decided to use the proceeds of his windfall to travel around Morocco while I was running the race. We agreed to meet up at the hotel in Ouarzazate, following the race.

I was terrified at the prospect of going back to the Sahara alone, so I decided that for my own psychological wellbeing, my second attempt at the MdS would need to feel like a completely different event. I didn't want to inadvertently re-create the same experience, along with the awful aftermath. I did a complete overhaul of everything race-related, including training, kit, nutrition and hydration – all my lessons learned has been captured in this book.

I also decided to train as much as possible on hills and trail. One evening, as I was coming home from work, I was trying to work out how I would build the leg strength required for running up and down the sand dunes. It occurred to me that although Central London was in short supply of sand dunes, I could find a proliferation of steps within each tube station. In fact, I lived five minutes away from a tube station!

One day, after returning home from work, I went to the station and added up a total of 77 steps. I reasoned that if I ran 10 sets of this flight of stairs, two or three times a week, carrying my complete MdS rucksack, I would soon build the leg strength required to run up the sand dunes. Pulling a large packet of chocolate chip cookies from my rucksack, I approached the most senior looking station guard, a man who looked like a cross between Barry White and B.A. Baracus from the A Team.

I waited for the commuters to pass through the security barriers and then made my move. As I invited Nigel to take a cookie, I shared my predicament in the most garbled way possible. *"I need your help! I've failed to complete a marathon across the Sahara. I only managed 75 miles and now I need to go back to finish it. I need to train for sand dunes by running up and down these stairs."* It was evident that he thought I had lost the plot. He looked up and down at my 5"1 frame and then suddenly, broke into a broad grin and suggested that I should come to the station after 9pm, after the commuter rush had subsided.

From that point onwards, Nigel allowed me through the barrier every Tuesday and Thursday, so that I could use the stairs to train. I had decided that with 10kg on my back, I would take the escalator down to the platform level and then run back up the long flight of steps. What I hadn't accounted for was that at that time, the tube station was still relatively busy. As I carried my rucksack on my back, complete with my Raidlight water bottles - which were strapped to each side of my chest like missiles, I looked like a laughable caricature of Lara Croft.

On one occasion, as I was running up the steep flight of stairs, I felt like my leg muscles would explode. I was so embarrassed about the ridiculousness of what I was doing, but I just carried on. As I looked to my right, I could see two Nigerian women, resplendent in Nigerian native outfits, complete with bright orange and gold head dresses, going up the escalator, clapping and beaming with huge smiles shouting, *"Keep going, you can do it!!!"* By the time I had reached the top of the flight of stairs for the tenth time that evening, every person in that tube station had broken out into a round of applause. This was not quite the inconspicuous training I had had in mind! Nevertheless, this sort of support, often from complete strangers, helped me to keep my spirits high and my determination strong.

Several months later, when faced with the realities of the race, the formalities of administration day and the race itself felt extremely familiar. In writing this book and deciding to go back to complete the race, I had analysed every single aspect of the Marathon des Sables. Although I met a lot of people in the camp and made many good friends, I knew that I had to remain focused. I simply could not afford to fail this race for a second time. My strategy for every single day was to wake up early enough to allow enough time to pack, complete the necessary foot preparations, eat and go through my cleaning and hygiene rituals. I started the race as close to the start line as possible and would run as much as I could, given that it was cooler in the mornings. This meant that during the peak heat of the day - between 12pm-3pm, I could afford to take a more relaxed pace.

It is difficult to explain how I felt as I started the race each morning. The first feeling was one of relief that I had made it this far. I knew that if I could keep going until the long stage, I was home dry. In my mind's eye, I kept visualising my end-of-race picture and kept thinking about how I would display my medal. I would also *feel* the medal hanging around my neck. As I focused more and more on my goal, I fell into an almost hypnotic state. It was almost as though the days and stages of the race merged into each other. My mind and body were in perfect unison; I was not in pain, nor was I afraid; I had pooled all of my resources to move seamlessly towards my goal. I was in flow.

Throughout the race, I was on high alert in terms of my own kit management, ensuring my feet were in good condition and that I was properly fuelled. This time, I developed a few blisters early on, but thankfully lost no toenails. Rather alarmingly, I lost a lot of feeling in both feet, apparently because I had badly bruised the nerve endings in my toes. I could feel nothing in my toes during the latter part of the race, or indeed for months afterwards. Even now, I only have partial feeling in my toes.

Completing the Marathon des Sables was a pretty surreal experience. Having crossed the finish line with the Welsh flag around my shoulders and a big medal hanging around my neck, I was given an ice-cold Coca-Cola. I walked into the camp and saw that a stage had been erected in the centre and the French Philharmonic orchestra was practicing their rendition of Adèle's *Rolling in the Deep*. I sat down, trying to digest the enormity of what my body and mind had been through. I had finally completed the toughest footrace on earth. I had closure.

There are a few moments in your life when you will come to the realisation that you have "arrived". These are moments where you recognise that there has been a significant and very positive shift between where you once were, compared to where you are now. Recognising that my self-image had improved and that I was achieving the things I had always wanted to achieve was a profound experience for me. I was and indeed am, *exactly* where I wanted to be.

It is beyond the scope of this book to describe the extent to which my first marathon changed my life. Needless to say, I learned the skills that helped me to develop an action-oriented mind-set - one that meant that I actively went about seeking the answers to much bigger questions about values and life purpose. I had designed my life in terms of challenges and experiences so well, that within the space of five years I had evolved from a novice runner to one that had run more than 20 marathons; climbed Mont Blanc, Kilimanjaro and Everest Base Camp; trekked Machu Picchu; white-water rafted along the Andes; learned to play the saxophone; performed stand-up comedy in front of 250 people; started my own business and raised more than £20,000 for different charities. The culmination of all of these challenges was the Marathon des Sables.

I sincerely believe that these achievements are just a small example of our potential as human beings. We are *all* capable of remarkable, outstanding achievements. In your quest to achieve, whether or not you are ready to run the Marathon des Sables, my advice is just this: don't put limitations on yourself and do not allow others to put limitations on you. Don't wait for the perfect time, because it doesn't exist. Your time is now.

RESOURCES

There are many resources available to you as your prepare for the Marathon des Sables. These resources are identified under the following sections:

- Hiking
- Training Races
- Kit and Stockists
- General Information

For information relating specifically to the Marathon des Sables, please go to www.darbaroud.com, which is the official site of the Marathon des Sables or www.marathondessables.co.uk, which is the entry site for British citizens.

Hiking

There are a number of organisations that you can join in order to hike in a group. I joined Meet Up (www.meetup.com) and the Long Distance Walkers Association (www.ldwa.org.uk).

As a London-based professional, I found the hiking groups through Meet Up to be extremely welcoming and convenient. You should look for groups that specialise in long-distance hikes (20 miles or more) at a fast pace (15-20mins/mile) over undulating terrain.

The Long Distance Walkers Association is very useful, since it provides a list of all of the various walking paths you can use in the UK and has a schedule of events listed by area and distance.

Training Races

MdS runners often incorporate specific races and multi-stage events as milestones in their training plans. Please note that the following list is indicative rather than exhaustive.

These events are important because they will give you a flavour of the scale of the challenge that MdS presents. They also provide you with a great opportunity to test out your equipment and supplies. However, you don't need to do every single race. I urge you to be selective to avoid risking unnecessary injury and expense.

Marathons
The 100 Marathon Club lists marathons in the UK and abroad (www.100marathonclub.org.uk), whilst SiEntries provides online entry for trail runs, ultra marathons, adventure races, etc. (www.sientries.co.uk)

Ultra-Marathons
The Ultra Marathon Running website provides a calendar list of all the ultra-marathon races and events in the UK (www.ultramarathonrunning.com). Some of the more popular races include:

The Round Rotherham: a trail event of 80 km/50 miles over an undulating route with, overall, 800m of ascension through the South Yorkshire Forest. (www.hmarston.co.uk)

The Bullock Smithy: a 56-mile course in the Peak District (www.bullocksmithy.com)

The Ridgeway 40 Ultra: a 40-mile ultra-marathon or walk along the ancient Ridgeway National Trail, which is reportedly the oldest road in Britain (www.beyondmarathon.com/event/the-ridgeway-40)

N.B. Beyond Marathon offer multi-day ultras, such as the Millennium Way Ultra and Gritstone Grind. If you are feeling overwhelmed, it is worth remembering that you could choose to use a walk or a walk/run strategy during these events.

Multi-Stage Ultra-Marathons
Some of the most popular multi-stage events include the 100 Mile Run Cotswold Challenge (www.100milerun.com), The Druids Challenge and the Pilgrims Challenge.

Some race organisers, such as XNRG (www.xnrg.co.uk) offer MdS packages at a reduced price, which are designed specifically to help you in your MdS training. Entering these more popular events will give you the opportunity to meet other MdS runners and form early friendships, which will be useful in terms of finding tent mates in Morocco.

Kit and Stockists

Specialist Running Shops
Some of the best-known specialist running shops include Runner's Need (www.runnersneed.com), Run & Become (www.runandbecome.com) and Sweatshop (www.sweatshop.co.uk). If you are a member of a running club, these stores often give 10%-15% discounts on your purchases. However, whilst these shops are a great resource for shoes, a basic kit and general advice - relating to injuries for example, I found that their knowledge of the specific challenges associated with multi-stage ultra-races was often very limited.

Specialist Ultra-Running Shops
As an ultra-runner, you will require specialist equipment that is not readily available from one of the aforementioned running shops. Specialist ultra-running suppliers are a fantastic resource, since they offer

advice based on personal experience and often have lots of samples of different items that you will need, such as rucksacks, sleeping bags and other similar items. Often you can try the items in-store, too.

In the event that you cannot physically go to these stores, you can always call and speak to someone who may well have completed the Marathon des Sables, or similar ultra-marathons, and can give you the benefit of their experience. Another advantage of these stores is that you can buy pretty much all of your equipment in one go.

I recommend Likeys (www.likeys.com) and MyRaceKit (www.myracekit.com). Likeys is based in North Wales and is run by Martin and Sue, who offer excellent advice and super-fast service. In fact, the lovely people at Likeys have come up with an extremely useful desert kit list, which can be found on their website. I thoroughly recommend speaking to someone if you are in any doubt about your specific requirements.

MyRaceKit is based in Essex and is run by Colin and Elisabet Barnes. Again, they provide fantastic service and valuable advice, since they are extremely experienced runners. You may also want to try other suppliers, such as Racing the Planet (www.uk.racingtheplanet.com) and Ultra Runner (www.ultra runner.com).

Foot Preparation - Tuf-Foot
Tuf-Foot is a specialist tanning solution for your feet. It is quite difficult to find this treatment, but you can buy it online from Culpeppers (www.culpeppers.co.uk). Don't be alarmed by the website, which says that they *"specialise in high quality dog wear for working, sled dog racing, special medical needs and pet dogs."* Tuf-foot is a recognised tanning solution for athletes too, to make their feet tough but supple.

Gaiter Specialists
If you live in London, I recommend Alex Shoe Repairs, which is based in Battersea (Tel: 020 7223 4931). The man who can fix gaiters to your shoes is called Kevin (not Alex!) and he is extremely skilled at fitting them for runners intending to head out to Morocco to run the Marathon des Sables.

Freeze Dried Food Suppliers
Likeys and MyRaceKit stock freeze-dried food, should you wish to take this option. Some of the most popular brands include Mountain House, Expedition Foods, Extreme Adventure Food and Extreme Food.

General Information

Websites
www.runultra.co.uk – an ultra-running discussion community, events and kit reviews.

www.myracekit.com/blog – advice and tips on ultra-running kits and equipment, run by Steve Dietrich, who is one of the UK MdS co-ordinators.

Blogs

Although there are plenty of MdS-related blogs on the internet, I would recommend being quite selective with what you choose to read. This is partly because the information can be conflicting, but also because you risk information overload.

I personally recommend the following blogs:

www.dannykendall.wordpress.com: elite athlete Danny Kendall.

www.justajog.com: regular runner Kate Lee, who keeps a diary account of her running and gives fantastic advice.

www.push2extreme.com: MdS Veteran Genis Pieterse, who provides incredibly detailed and high-quality research based on the experience of MdS runners.

www.ultrarunnereli.com: elite British athlete and co-owner of MyRaceKit, Elizabet Barnes.

You will also find a complete list of MdS blogs on the MdS website.

Facebook Group

The official MdS Facebook group follows the naming convention "MDS UK Runners (+ the year of your race)". It is a closed group, administered by one of the UK MdS volunteers, which means that your entry for MdS for the current year must be verified before you can join. Please contact the MdS organisers for details.

Podcasts

www.iancorless.org: Ian Corless regularly interviews elite runners, nutritionists and physiotherapists to gain a diverse range of perspectives of the MdS. This is a very useful resource for you to access, if you have time.

Films

The Toughest Footrace on Earth is a cult film for those who are running the MdS for the first time. It describes the journey that Olympic rower James Cracknell took to become the highest ranked Briton to run the MdS, finishing the race in 12th place.

Race Photography

For photographer information, you should contact the MdS organisation directly. Official pictures will be available to purchase after the event, via the MdS website, although these are quite limited in terms of number. I recommend Ian Corless (www.iancorless.org) should you want someone to follow you and take many pictures exclusively of you, throughout the race.

You can also take your own camera or video device. Just before you leave for Morocco, the organisers will email you and ask that you declare any video device that you intend to take with you, for copyright and privacy reasons.

MdS Insurance

Sutcliffe and Co. (www.sutcliffeinsurance.co.uk) and Dogtag (www.dogtag.co.uk) are the most popular insurance brokers for MdS.

APPENDIX A: EXAMPLE TRAINING PLAN

Irrespective of whether your goal is to complete or compete, your training programme must be designed in such a way that it: 1) allows you to run at least 20 miles, walking when you have to; 2) with your MdS rucksack, which contains your anticipated weight and actual equipment; 3) across varied and undulating terrain; and 4) over a number of consecutive days. Figure 22 represents the training plan I used to achieve these goals.

I recommend that you consider the principles in the relevant section of this book and create a plan that also recognises the following points:

- Every run should have a purpose to prevent your fitness reaching a plateau.
- Use weekends for specific types of training. For most people, this is time off work. Hills before a long run is not an ideal strategy, but do what you can when you can. You may also choose to alternate long, slow runs with long, hilly hikes.
- Add weight in increments of 1kg once you reach 10 miles in your training plan. Only do this if you are injury-free and training is progressing well.
- Aim for a backpack weighing 8-9kg for the actual race, but train with more to build your strength.
- Carry as much of your actual kit as soon as possible and decide where to distribute items on your rucksack for easy access.
- Test out that food items you intend to take with you to the Sahara during your training runs.
- Listen to your body and take rests when you need them.
- Ideally rest periods should be complete rest, but depending on how your body responds to training, it can also mean active rest, with alternative exercise to running such as yoga, pilates or cycling.
- Include milestone races and multi-stage events. Although I didn't do the formal Druids Challenge and Pilgrims Challenge, I ran the routes twice with a group of friends.

Month	Wk	Rucksack weight (KG)	Mon Easy	Tue Intervals	Wed REST	Thu Tempo	Fri REST	Sat Hills	Sun Long, slow run	TOTAL MILES (M)
SEPT 1	1		4	5	REST	6	REST	6	3	24
	2		4	5	REST	7	REST	6	4	26
	3		4	5	REST	7	REST	6	5	27
	4		4	5	REST	REST	Druids Challenge route check (84m)			93
OCT 2	5		5	5	REST	8	REST	6	7	31
	6		5	5	REST	9	REST	6	8	33
	7		5	5	REST	9	REST	6	9	34
	8	1	5	5	REST	10	REST	6	10	36
NOV 3	9	2	4	5	REST	REST	Druids Challenge route check (84m)			93
	10	2	6	5	REST	11	REST	6	12	40
	11	3	6	5	REST	11	REST	6	14	42
	12	3	6	5	REST	12	REST	6	16	45
DEC 4	13	4	6	5	REST	12	REST	6	18	47
	14	4	6	5	REST	13	REST	Pilgrim's Challenge (66m)		77
	15	5	6	5	REST	13	REST	6	20	50
	16	6	6	5	REST	13	REST	6	20	50
JAN 5	17	7	6	5	REST	13	REST	6	20	50
	18	8	6	5	REST	13	REST	Pilgrim's Challenge (66m)		77
	19	9	6	5	REST	13	REST	6	REST	30
	20	10	20	20	20	20	20	REST	REST	100
FEB 6	21	10	6	5	REST	13	REST	6	16	46
	22	10	REST	5	REST	5	REST	50	REST	60
	23	10	REST	REST	REST	6	REST	6	REST	12
	24	10	6	5	REST	6	REST	6	16	39
MAR 7	25	10	REST	5	REST	5	REST	50	REST	60
	26	10	REST	REST	7	7	REST	7	7	28
	27	10	REST	5	REST	6	REST	3	REST	14
	28	10	3	REST	REST	3	REST	3	REST	9
APR 8	29	NA	**** RACE WEEK ****							

Figure 22: Example training plan

In Figure 22, you can see a row called "Types of Training Run". This variation is to help prevent a plateau in fitness.

From this plan, you can see that I achieved the aforementioned objectives at specific points within the training plan. Specifically:

- Objective 1, to be able to run 20 miles, was achieved from week 15 (Sunday) onwards.
- Objective 2, to train with anticipated weight and actual equipment, started in week 8 and continued to build cumulatively until week 20, after which the weight that I ran with remained consistently at 10kg.
- Objective 3, to run across varied and undulating terrain, began in week 8, on the long, slow run on Sundays and continued throughout my training programme.
- Objective 4, to run back-to-back long runs began at week 20, with 5 x 20m back-to-back runs.

The 5 x 20 mile runs represented the peak of my training. If you choose to follow this plan, proceed carefully; listen to your body and see how you feel after each day. If you develop niggling pain or injuries, stop and rest. You can split 20m into 2 x 10m if it is easier.

Additionally, Figure 22 shows 2 x 50 mile runs. I split each 50 mile run into 2 x 25 mile runs. This was definitely the most gruelling part of my training, but I recommend having this particular milestone in your plan, because it will give you a tremendous amount of confidence for the long stage of the MdS.

APPENDIX B: EXAMPLE KEY MILESTONE PLAN

Figure 23 is an example of the key milestone plan I created to manage my MdS race preparation. Capturing milestones in this way allowed me to easily track my own progress - not just in terms of training, but for all aspects of the race such as kit, food, admin and final checks.

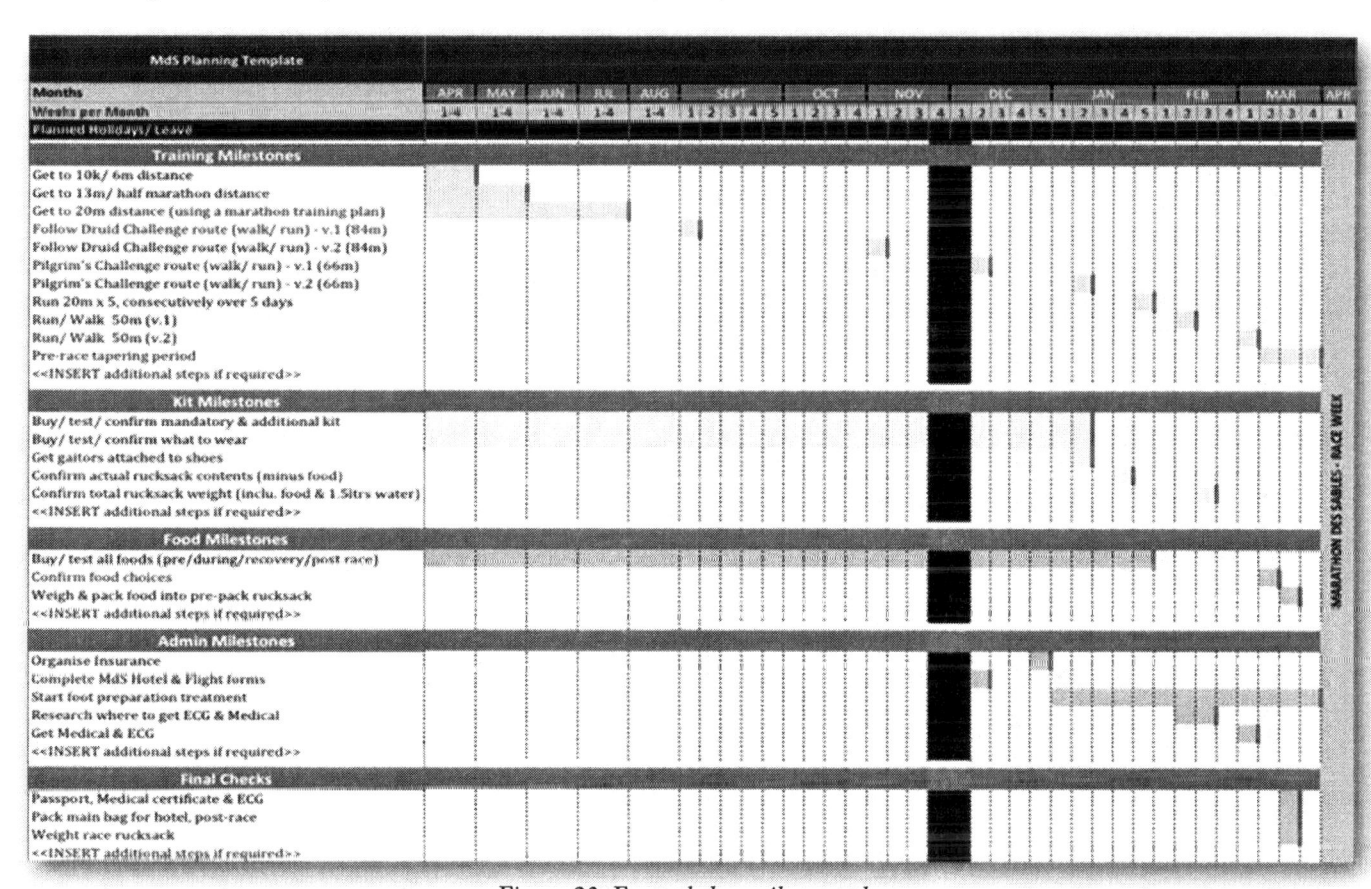

Figure 23: Example key milestone plan

General notes

- The left-hand column lists a series of milestones, categorised under training, kit, food, admin and final checks. I have included the key milestones under these categories and encourage you to identify further milestones that you think are necessary for your own MdS preparations. I recommend keeping these as high-level as possible, so that the plan remains manageable.
- Across the top, the plan identifies the months that make up the plan, split by weeks, with the exception of Apr-Aug. This is purely for ease of presentation for the purposes of this book. I have included a generous date-range to show how a person might progress from non-runner to ultra-runner. You may already be a runner or ultra-runner, in which case you can modify or shorten the training date range to suit your needs.
- I have included planned holidays and leave to allow for realistic planning.

Notes for Training milestones

- The training milestones can be created using the information contained in the Training Strategy chapter of this book.
- The milestones must reflect your own specific training needs.
- Note that in this plan, certain milestones - e.g. "Follow Druid Challenge route" were completed over a long weekend.
- Weekly training milestones are not reflected in this high-level plan. I used the training plan outlined in Figure 22 to track my training progress on a week-by-week basis.
- I started running with rucksack weight at the end of October and incrementally increased this weight over the following months. Details of the approach I used are indicated in Figure 22.

Notes for Kit milestones

- The testing of kit includes both consideration of suitability but also of the weight implications on your total rucksack weight.

Notes for Food milestones

- Confirming food choices means that you have considered your specific calorific requirements, the calorific value derived from your choices and rucksack weight implications of your food choices.

Notes for Admin milestones

- The specific dates of some of the admin-related milestones will depend on the dates given by the MdS organisation. For example, at the time of writing, a runner's ECG and medical were only accepted if both were completed in the few weeks prior to the race. The forms for hotel, flight details etc. will be sent to you by the organisation via email, which means that your plan will need to be adjusted accordingly.

Finally, it's important to manage your own expectations with regards to planning. No plan is perfect and there is bound to be slippage - maybe due to injury or work/ family commitments. I went through many, many iterations of my plan, so please don't be alarmed if you experience the same thing. This plan will give you a clear overview of the scope of activities that MdS preparation involves, which in turn, will significantly reduce any anxiety!

APPENDIX C: EXAMPLE KIT LIST

Figure 24 shows how I kept track of my MdS kit.

Category	Item	Comments	Status
Mandatory Kit	Rucksack or equivalent		Bought
Mandatory Kit	Sleeping bag		Bought
Mandatory Kit	Head torch with spare batteries		Bought
Mandatory Kit	10 safety pins		Bought
Mandatory Kit	Compass, with 1° or 2° precision		Bought
Mandatory Kit	Lighter (you have to carry this, even if you're not intending to using cooking fuel)		Bought
Mandatory Kit	Whistle		Bought
Mandatory Kit	Knife with metal blade		Bought
Mandatory Kit	Topical disinfectant		Bought
Mandatory Kit	Anti-venom pump		Bought
Mandatory Kit	A signalling mirror		Bought
Mandatory Kit	One aluminium survival sheet		Bought
Mandatory Kit	One tube of sun cream,		Bought
Mandatory Kit	200 euros or equivalent in foreign		Bought
Mandatory Kit	Passport		Bought
Mandatory Kit	Credit cards		Bought
Toiletries	Toilet roll		Bought
Toiletries	Toothbrush & paste		Bought
Toiletries	Hand sanitser		Bought
First Aid	Sunscreen	Also Mandatory Kit	Bought
First Aid	Plasters	Doc trotters can provide extra	Bought
First Aid	Topical disinfectant	Also Mandatory Kit	Bought
First Aid	Wet wipes (15)		Bought
First Aid	Lip balm		Bought
First Aid	Zinc oxide tape x 2		Bought
First Aid	Immodium		Bought
First Aid	Ibuprofen	Doc trotters can provide extra	Bought
First Aid	Paracetamol	Doc trotters can provide extra	Bought
First Aid	Foam ear plugs		Bought
First Aid	Body glide		Bought
Sleep System	Tyvek ("boiler") suit		Bought
Sleep System	Helly Hanson base layer		Bought
Sleep System	Sleeping bag		Bought

Figure 24: Example kit list

Firstly, I identified all of the items that I would need to take with me for the duration of the Marathon des Sables. I then categorised them as follows: Mandatory Kit, Toiletries, First Aid, Sleep System, Clothing, Running Kit, Gadgets, Hydration, Nutrition. The contents of your list will undoubtedly look quite different to mine, which is why I haven't shown all of mine here.

For more information on what you will need to take with you, you should refer to the relevant chapters of this book.

Listing your kit items in this way will ensure that nothing is missed. It will also allow you to identify the status of items (e.g. bought/ to buy) and to weed out items that are adding unnecessary weight. The weight of these items will add up significantly, so you will have to determine how to limit overall pack weight. You will also have to make trade-offs between items. It is a good idea to start using as much of the kit as possible, to quickly determine what is a "must have" item versus a "nice-to-have" item.

APPENDIX D: EXAMPLE MENU BREAKDOWN

Figure 25 shows how I tracked my food items for MdS. The grey rows at the bottom of these tables show total calories for all items, along with total weight of all items in grams.

I created tables like those below, for each day of the race. I have included three tables here for illustrative purposes. Your menu requirements will be quite different to mine, depending on your personal preferences, gender and size.

It's important to note that even though there is technically no race on day 7, the race rules stipulate that you must also carry 2,000 kcals for the 7th day.

Day 4 (Wednesday)	
Item	Kcals
Brie Bar	755
Dates & Rasins Mix	310
Rego Recovery Shake	184
Biltong	204
Dr. Kargs x 3	342
Nature Valley Crunch Bar	192
TOTAL (Kcals)	1987
TOTAL WEIGHT (G)	490

Day 5 (Thursday)	
Item	Kcals
Brie Bar	755
Dates & Rasins Mix	310
Rego Recovery Shake	184
Biltong	204
Dr. Kargs x 3	342
Nature Valley Crunch Bar	192
TOTAL (Kcals)	1987
TOTAL WEIGHT (G)	490

Day 6 (Friday)	
Item	Kcals
Brie Bar	755
Dates & Rasins Mix	310
Rego Recovery Shake	184
Biltong	204
Dr. Kargs x 2	228
Nature Valley Crunch Bar	192
TOTAL (Kcals)	1873
TOTAL WEIGHT (G)	465

Figure 25: Example menu breakdown (3 days, only)

I recommend that you create a table for each day of the race and populate the table by food item. As you do this, it makes sense to also list the calories provided by each item and its weight. If you are intending to take pre-packaged items, you should note that the weight listed on the packaging usually relates to the contents of the packet. It does not factor in the weight of the packaging. However, you can re-pack items to reduce the weight of the food packs overall.

Figure 26 shows a table of every ration pack that I took for MdS, broken down by kcals per day and total weight per ration pack. This table is informed by the information from all 'per day' tables previously described in Appendix D.

As in the previous tables, the grey row at the bottom of this table totals up all calories and weight of all food packs. This table shows that the total weight of all food packs combined was 3.2kg and that the total kcals of all food packs combined was 14,117 kcals.

Totals (Weight & Kcals)		
Days	Kcals/Day	Weight/Day
Day 1	2,090	455g
Day 2	1,873	465g
Day 3	2,090	455g
Day 4	1,987	490g
Day 5	1,987	490g
Day 6	2,000	465g
Day 7	2,090	465g
Total	14,117 kcals	3.2kg

Figure 26: Breakdown of total food packs (weight & kcals)

As part of the checks on administration day, you will be required to provide evidence that you are carrying sufficient calories for the duration of the race. Once food items have been tested and confirmed, you can create a table for each food pack and tape it onto the pack. If you are proficient at excel, I recommend using this to create all tables. You can then amend the spread sheet as many times as you like before saving the final version and printing off a copy, ready for review by race organisers.

Creating this kind of table will allow you to track the calorific value of food items consumed during MdS. It will also allow you to make an assessment of value against relative weight of each food item. Please note that not all calories are equal and that the decision to take more protein or carbohydrate calories will be dependent on individual racing strategy, as well as personal requirements such as height, build, metabolic rate etc. Please refer to chapter 7 of this book for more information on food and nutrition.

APPENDIX E: PHOTOGRAPHS

Figure 27: Al fresco toilet stop, on the way to camp

Figure 28: Administration day and kit check

Figure 29: Main luggage being taken back to the hotel on Administration day

Figure 30: Race Director, Patrick Bauer giving one of his many pre-race speeches

Figure 31: At the start line

Figure 32: The elite athletes lined up at the start

Figure 33: Packing at 7am, pre-race

Figure 34: Line-up of some of the support vehicles

Figure 35: The medical tent, for post-run support

Figure 36: Example of a jebel

Figure 37: An indication of the varied terrain (1)

Figure 38: An indication of the varied terrain (2)

TABLE OF FIGURES

Figure 1: With Sir Ranulph Fiennes, a day before the start of MdS 2015 20
Figure 2: Comparison between different race aspirations 25
Figure 3: Example schedule depending on race strategy 26
Figure 4: Comparison between my race strategies 28
Figure 5: Example 16 week marathon training plan 29
Figure 6: Relationship between weekly distance and performance in the countdown to the race 31
Figure 7: Relationship between long run frequency and MdS race position 32
Figure 8: The GPS device that replaced the distress flare in 2015 41
Figure 9: The contents of my MdS rucksack 50
Figure 10: Review of example rucksack 1 51
Figure 11: Review of example rucksack 2 52
Figure 12: Review of example rucksack 3 53
Figure 13: Example food packs, by day 63
Figure 14: Example contents of one ration pack 63
Figure 15: An example water card 67
Figure 16: The effects of poor foot management 72
Figure 17: Diagram of a compass 77
Figure 18: Home-made heat acclimatisation chamber 78
Figure 19: Layout of camp and location by nationality 82
Figure 20: Immediately after crossing the finish line 88
Figure 21: My MdS medal and special memories 88
Figure 22: Example training plan 102
Figure 23: Example key milestone plan 105
Figure 24: Example kit list 109
Figure 25: Example menu breakdown (3 days, only) 111
Figure 26: Breakdown of total food packs (weight & kcals) 112
Figure 27: Al fresco toilet stop, on the way to camp 113
Figure 28: Administration day and kit check 113
Figure 29: Main luggage being taken back to the hotel on Administration day 114
Figure 30: Race Director, Patrick Bauer giving one of his many pre-race speeches 114
Figure 31: At the start line 115
Figure 32: The elite athletes lined up at the start 115
Figure 33: Packing at 7am, pre-race 116
Figure 34: Line-up of some of the support vehicles 116

Figure 35: The medical tent, for post-run support 117
Figure 36: Example of a jebel 117
Figure 37: An indication of the varied terrain (1) 118
Figure 38: An indication of the varied terrain (2) 118

INDEX

A
Achilles Tendonitis, 70
Administration Day, 84
Ankle Sprains, 71
Anti-Venom Pump, 44
Airport (At the), 83

B
Blisters, 71
Body Glide, 46
Bottles, 48

C
Camp, At the, 84
Camp Layout, 82
Common Injuries, 69
Compass, 43, 76, 77
Cooking Equipment, 47
Cross-Training, 34

D
Dehydration, 65
Duct Tape, 47

E
Entrants, Types of 19,
Esbit Cubes (fuel), 47
Example Rucksack Contents (Review of), 51, 52, 53

F
Calories (Fat Calories vs. Carbohydrate Calories), 59
Filming and Photography, 79
Finishing (the Race), 87
First Aid, 46

Flow, 2
Food & Hydration, 59
Food Ideas (Additional), 64
Food Options, 60
Friends and Family, 79

G
Gaiters, 57
Glow Stick, 41
GoPro Camera, 48
GPS Watch, 57

H
Head Torch, 43
Headwear, 55
Heat Acclimatisation, 78
Hip Strap, 42

I
Injury Prevention & Management, 69
ITBS, 71

K
Knife, 44
Kristin Armstrong, 3

L
Lao Tzu, 2
Life After MdS, 89
Lighter, 44
Lip Balm, 46
Long-Sleeved Top, 48
Long Stage (The), 87

M
Mandatory Equipment, 39
Mandatory Kit List, 39
Marathon Training Plan, 28
MdS Facts, 81
Medical & ECG, 76
Mental Strength Training, 35
Mihaly Csikszentmihalyi, 2
Miles to Kilometres Conversion, 78

Milestone Races and Hikes, 33
Minimum Calorie Requirements, 59
Morocco (In), 83
Multi-Stage Events, 34
Multi-Stage Racing, 18
My Nutritional Plan, 61

N
Navigation, 76
NLP, 36
Nutrition, during Training, 61
Nutrition, for the Race, 62
Nutritional Plan, 61

P
Patellar Tendonitis, 70
Performance Implications, 31
Plantar Fasciitis, 70
Powders, 62
Preparing Your Feet, 76
Pre-Race Preparation, 75
Pulled Muscles, 71

R
Race Countdown & Completion, 81
Race Logistics, 81
Race Picture, 87
Race Rules and Regulations, 19
Race Stages, 18
Race Strategies (Comparison Between 2014 and 2015), 28
Race Tactics, 75
Ration Packs (Example), 62
Road Book, 40
Rucksack Contents, 50
Weight-Saving Changes (Recommended), 51, 52, 53
Runner's Knee, 69
Running Shirt, 56
Running Tights, 56

S
Sand Training, 34
Shin Splints, 71
Shoes (Trail or Road), 48

Shoulder Straps, 42
Signalling Mirror, 45
Sleep System, 47
Sleeping Bag, 42
Slippers, 48
Socks, 49, 56
Solar Charger, 49
Spare Batteries, 43
Sun Cream, 45
Sunglasses, 55

T
Temperature, 18
Terrain (Finding Appropriate), 32
Toilet Roll, Wipes and Sanitiser, 45
Topical Disinfectant, 44
Tracking, 79
Trail or Road Shoes, 48
Training Groups, 33
Training Plan (Considerations), 29
Training Plans (Alternative), 31
Training Principles, 27
Training Strategy, 23

U
Useful Tips, 83, 84, 85

V
Vaseline, 46

W
Walking (Running or), 24
Walking Poles, 48
Weight Distribution(Back-to-Front), 42
Whistle, 44